Prof M. Ángeles Cerezo is chair of psychology at the University of Valencia, Spain. Her research publications focus on family relationships, especially early interaction with babies as a predictor of child attachment. She has been a visiting professor at universities in Ireland, USA and Canada. Applying the science of babies, she developed a universal program to support parents and their babies, to promote their well-being and emotional security (Spanish and English versions: PAPMI© & PCPS™). Her university recognised this applied facet of her work through the Social Innovation spin-off Instituto Psicológico de la Infancia y la Familia (IPINFA) where she is scientific director.

To my parents, the memory of whom is
my constant companion.

M. Ángeles Cerezo

IF BABIES COULD TALK

A WINDOW INTO THEIR AMAZING
EMOTIONAL LIFE

AUSTIN MACAULEY PUBLISHERS™
LONDON • CAMBRIDGE • NEW YORK • SHARJAH

Copyright © M. Ángeles Cerezo (2020)

The right of M. Ángeles Cerezo to be identified as an author of this work has been asserted by her in accordance with section 77 and 78 of the Copyright, Designs and Patents Act 1988.

All rights reserved. No part of this publication may be reproduced, stored in a retrieval system, or transmitted in any form or by any means, electronic, mechanical, photocopying, recording, or otherwise, without the prior permission of the publishers.

Any person who commits any unauthorised act in relation to this publication may be liable to criminal prosecution and civil claims for damages.

Austin Macauley is committed to publishing works of quality and integrity. In this spirit, we are proud to offer this book to our readers; however, the story, the experiences, and the words are the author's alone.

This is a work of fiction. Names, characters, businesses, places, events, locales, and incidents are either the products of the author's imagination or used in a fictitious manner. Any resemblance to actual persons, living or dead, or actual events is purely coincidental.

A CIP catalogue record for this title is available from the British Library.

ISBN 9781528977562 (Paperback)
ISBN 9781528977586 (ePub e-book)

www.austinmacauley.com

First Published (2020)
Austin Macauley Publishers Ltd
25, Canada Square
Canary Wharf
London
E14 5LQ

Converting an idea into something tangible like this book is a personal journey that has been made in the best of company. To those people who have accompanied me, I offer my gratitude. Our conversations, their comments, their patience while my little obsession lasted, and above all, their encouragement and trust remain in my memory connected to these pages. Special thanks to my family: my husband, Kieran, who always encourages me to write and my children, Clara and Jaime, whose comments on this work made me reflect and improve it. Finally, there have been some very special companions on this trip, the babies and their families who, for so many years, have been teaching me the meaning of what I studied and researched. To all of them, thank you.

Table of Contents

Foreword	**11**
Introduction	**13**
We Want Our Children to Do Well	15
What If Babies Could Talk?	18
1. The Good Shadow of My Great Tree	**23**
A Daddy with Two Faces	25
What Luck! Mummy Works at a Nursery School	27
What Is Happening Here?	29
What These Stories Teach Us	32
2. Knock Knock, Is Anyone There?	**33**
Mummy Is Not Responding	35
My mum Is So Pretty	37
Very Noisy Mum and Dad	39
What Is Happening Here?	41
What These Stories Teach Us?	44
3. Information Flood! Give Me a Break, Please	**47**
My Mum and Dad Take Extra Care of Me	49
Mummy and Daddy Want the Very Best for Me	51
What Is Happening Here?	54
What These Stories Teach Us?	57

4. I Miss You, Where Are You?	**59**
Mummy Smartphonehands	61
Mummy and Her Seat-less Pram	63
What Is Happening Here?	66
What These Stories Teach Us?	69
5. I Can't Explain Myself Properly Yet: Even I Don't Understand Me	**71**
My Mother Has the Solution for All My Troubles	73
I'm Always in the Air	75
What Is Happening Here?	78
What These Stories Teach Us?	80
6. There's a Lot of Noise There. Can You Hear Me?	**83**
Mummy's Hope	84
Bad Experiences	87
My Two Dinners	89
What Is Happening Here?	91
What These Stories Teach Us?	96
7. Don't Push Me Too Much or Too Little…Just the Right Amount!	**99**
Mummy Wants Me to Be Her Baby Forever	101
Mummy and Daddy Are Super-Proud of Me	104
Older or Younger, Which Is It?	105
What Is Happening Here?	108
What These Stories Teach Us?	111
Recapitulation	**113**

Foreword

This book has come about after a process that now, looking back, seems almost natural. It has been preceded by decades devoted to study and research into the emotional development of children – that development in which their human mind emerges within a relationship with those who bring them into the world. But also after decades of learning from mothers and fathers whom I have accompanied, in one way or another, on their personal journey of connection and understanding with their children. And together with all this, the experience of having raised my children with the doubts and questions that motherhood brings.

So, one beautiful spring morning on the way to work, while I was thinking about these things, two mothers with their babies passed by. I looked at the infants and imagined them talking in a "mysterious code" about their emotional life and how they were trying to make sense of a world so new and unknown to them. That fantasy, which made me smile, stayed in my mind and for a while I found myself imagining them having chat after chat that expressed, in the most "naïve" words, important scientific topics and their practical application.

I felt the need to share what we know today with the people who have babies in their care but also with all those interested in the Big Bang that is the awakening of the mind and the first months of human life. The affective experiences of babies in their connection with us help them understand and manage their emotions. Perhaps one of the most important messages is that good emotional regulation is essential to be able to develop, subsequently, adequate cognitive functioning. Often, from the beginning, the emphasis is on everything that is "learning". However, as science teaches us today, our babies "learn how to learn" in the foundational emotional stage to which these pages are devoted.

Introduction

The arrival of a child changes our lives. This change is preceded by a period of waiting, full of anticipation, and the wait is particularly special for the mother who experiences the gestation in her own body. At long last, the moment arrives and we have the child in our arms, it seems almost incredible. How often, with a newborn baby, do we look at their little hands with all of their tiny fingers and it seems marvellous and wonderful to us? This is a masterpiece of Nature!

When we finally return home with the baby in our arms, with all the congratulations and a flood of new experiences, we have the impression that this is a decisive moment and it is natural to feel a little uncertain at this point. Sometimes, we mothers find that our hormones are agitated; we are sad and tearful without knowing why and without the time or space to deal with it. *In fact, having a child is considered to be a highly stressful transitional event in life, one that in some cases can disturb a person's balance. Therefore, all parents of newborns require support.*

We want to be the best for our child, who is so precious and so helpless. We feel the great responsibility involved in being everything for this baby and being there to nurture their development. We feel that we will do everything in our power for their well-being and happiness, give this child the very best of ourselves. But then there is the reality of everyday life; the baby cries or does not cry, sleeps or does not sleep... what are we to do? Furthermore, we are exhausted, both physically and emotionally. Where do we start? What if we get things all wrong?

All our attention is focused on things related to parenting and children, because we have a thousand doubts and we need to know about a matter that is as important as life itself. Friends and family, our own and our partner's, all give opinions and advice. In addition, thanks to technology and our e-connected world, we have endless sources of information and a range of answers, sometimes conflicting ones, to our many questions. Never before have there been so many guides, blogs, books, conferences, YouTube videos... that even create fashionable trends.

Today, the information about bringing up children has become polarised due to an explosion of information about ways of parenting that rediscover the importance of attachment, respect, natural approaches, emotions, the child's freedom and many other factors. These ways of parenting often position themselves as being in contrast with what is considered "usual" or "conventional" parenting. Regardless of the different labels that each orientation chooses, the panorama on parenting nowadays has two main fronts: parenting organised with absolute adaptation to the child versus adaptation of the child to the adult.

Let us start with the adaptation of the child to the adult. There are women and men who want everything to remain the same when they become parents. Having doubts is understandable because adaptation to a new situation is a personal process and space is needed to express fears for the loss of the known and the transition to the new. However, it is not realistic to expect that everything will continue as before because it is not "before", anymore, it is now; there were one or two of us and now there are three or four. It is a bit like when we hear from someone who gets involved in a romantic relationship but wants to continue living exactly the way they did when they had no partner. Applying this to the parenting situation, we cannot go on expecting the baby to "behave well", not to bother us, to adapt to our needs and schedules, to be able to continue as if nothing, or almost nothing had changed.

There is a variant, which is not so much wanting everything to stay the same as before the baby arrived, but rather wanting the child to behave in the same way as we do as quickly as possible. The result is very similar, to press the accelerator so that the child gets older quicker.

At the other extreme, there are people who, when they become parents, are completely absorbed in their new role in a *sustained* manner. Of course, during the first weeks an absolute adaptation to the baby is required. We have to spend 24 hours a day caring for the baby and looking after their needs, even deferring our own basic needs, which inevitably take a back seat. However, those first few weeks are a transitional stage. When we refer to mothers and fathers who are absorbed in their new role in a *sustained way*, this means that they take this on with a belief that the child is wise by nature. Therefore, the child will set the times according to their wishes and needs in everything that concerns them.

From this perspective, this form of parenting is considered optimal because it will provide the child with the confidence and security they need for their development and happiness. Although the commitment of these parents is praiseworthy, the reality is that it indicates a remarkable lack of understanding of how the human mind works in the first three years of life.

We Want Our Children to Do Well

The paradox and ultimately the good news is that both kinds of parents agree on the goal of this journey that begins with the birth of the baby. We want our children to be well, be happy, relate well to others, be independent, cope with life, ride the ups and downs, and not succumb to any setbacks that may arrive. What mother or father, looking at their newborn, would not want these for their child? So, this is a journey with your son or daughter that reaches its destination when they, as an adult, look at you in the eye, making their own decisions and living their own life. You will continue to be that person's mother or father, but your main task has concluded.

So, even though they agree on the destination of their journey, the difference between the two approaches mentioned above is in the word "how". It is how we fathers and mothers believe we can reach that cherished final destination.

This "how" brings with it all our beliefs about what "should be" as well as all our own experiences of having been daughters or sons, sisters or brothers... These beliefs, in turn, activate the deepest of our emotional intricacies, our philosophy of life: a whole microcosm.

From that microcosm in which we live, attention is paid to one piece of information or to another, as we identify ourselves, more or less with it. This information comes to us as something shared, supported by others who are at the same stage of life, and the sensation of being "one of many" always provides a sense of belonging, of being part of a group; it offers some security precisely when we are feeling more insecure. Furthermore, if the position is reinforced with the ancestral contrast of being "good or bad", the adherence to our "principles" becomes more solid. We are the good parents because we educate our children; teach them to behave, lead them along the right path, while, the others, the bad parents, who leave them without guidance, who are always at their service, who teach them to be selfish tyrants... Or, on the other side, we are the good parents: altruistic, respectful, lovers of the "natural", of affection, of attachment, against those bad parents who are selfish, conventional, behaviourist, child handlers...

Interestingly, despite the fact that the "how to get there" of these two approaches is so different, deep down, they share two aspects. One, both view their child as an adult. Two, both fail to set out different spaces of relationship. *These aspects, as we now know, do not favour a healthy relationship with our children and interfere with their development and emotional well-being.*

Indeed, parents who choose to remain in the initial phase in a sustained manner, waiting for the child to decide the when and the how, believe that the child is like them: an adult who knows their own needs and what suits them, and the parents are just there to give it to them. On the other hand, when it comes to those parents who expect a well-behaved child too soon, when the baby does not do this, they think it is due to a deliberate intention to make their lives difficult. These parents are also considering, from another perspective, the child as an adult who knows what they are doing. However, this is not the case, *babies do not function like adults: they have to get there but they are many miles from their destination. Treating them as adults makes their journey very difficult. It is us who are the adults.*

What can we say about setting out spaces for different relationships? If there is nothing more to life than serving the child and their wishes and needs, or, on the contrary, if nothing has changed here and we are as we were before, the necessary relocation within our lives that the situation requires has not taken place. That is, in both cases, there is no differentiation in the spaces required for relationships. It is as if we start a relationship and then put everything into orbit around it or, on the contrary, we intend to continue as if nothing has changed. The reality is that the relationship determines a new situation requiring us to reinvent ourselves by creating a common space, while negotiating and maintaining our own individual space.

Now with a baby, in addition to the space that needs to be created for the new arrival, it is also necessary to redefine our own spaces, as individuals, as a couple and as a family. This allows us to charge our batteries to serve our babies better. We will have more to give them. At the same time, this experience of parenthood gives us other energies that transfer to other spheres of our reality as individuals in a state of constant development.

What should we do then? Perhaps, in all these efforts to find the best way to raise our babies we overlook the principal characters in this story. The truth is that in comparison with other areas of knowledge, scientific knowledge about the development of babies has only been consolidated in relatively recent times. However, nowadays we have very valuable, demonstrated information that we should use as a reference. With it as a guide and bearing the thought in mind that each parent is different, it can help us to create our own parenting style. This book is about looking at their world in order to know babies better. It grants them "superpowers" for a while, only for as long as it takes to read these pages, and it gives them a voice.

What If Babies Could Talk?

What about the babies? They are the main characters in this story, and if they could speak to us, in a kind of virtual world, what would they tell us about their experiences? They would say that they must be cared for with *unconditional love*, but also that it is necessary for them to have the *guidance and leadership* of these grown-ups. They would say that they have needs, but they do not always know what they need, and what they show as a need is not always the best thing for them. Therefore, the grown-ups in their lives, attentive, loving and patient, have to establish a way of life, knowing what is required and what is right at that time. Babies would say that this gives them a kind of scaffolding that allows them to progress towards greater regulation of their emotions, based on their parents' own regulation. *They would also say that they do not feel good if the people who care for and protect them do not feel well within themselves because they do not have their own spaces where they can recover their energy.*

If babies "talked" they would shed a lot of light on their world. If they could speak to us, all that energy we put into caring for them and loving them would be better channelled towards the goal we have had since the day we decided to bring them into this world. The goal that they become happy and useful people, for themselves and for others, thus contributing to a better world.

Let us imagine a magical space where babies communicate with each other. Only when we enter into this space, stealthily, we can be silent witnesses to what happens there. Babies refer to their speech with adults as CCG (Code for Communicating with Grown-ups), something that they learn with effort when they try to communicate with their parents. Likewise, as a part of their communication with the adult world out there, sometimes they describe their cries as "code one", "code two" or "code three", depending on what they think is happening to them: hunger, tiredness, pain…

This text has been divided into seven chapters based on different experiences that babies can have in their eagerness to communicate with that special person who, for them, initially constitutes "the world". These "talks" have been structured as dialogues in which each of our main characters "talks" with another baby; what she or he tells us always occupies the right part of these magical pages, while on the left, we see what their little friend says. The stories that we overhear acquire their full meaning in the section 'What Is Happening Here?' and each chapter concludes with a reflection on "What These Stories Teach Us".

The first chapter, 'The Good Shadow of My Great Tree', shows us the naive conversations that Rose and Jack, two children both aged one, have with their respective companions, other babies, in which we glimpse some stories that can be understood fully in the section 'What Is Happening Here?'.

This chapter presents that part of the age of life in which the human being, through the experiences with the "special person", has already developed not only a certain idea or representation of how predictable, or not the world is but also of who they are in relation to that world. This age of life is the first birthday.

After the child's first birthday, they stand up, ready for the great journey of their life. *The child will travel this journey with the luggage of their accumulated experience of the relationship with this special person. That experience will have allowed them to develop a sense of security, cultivated under a good shadow from the large tree that stands over them, or perhaps a feeling of insecurity, the result of a very small shadow.*

The subsequent chapters look at what happens before we arrive at that stage, that is, the establishment of that relationship from birth. More specifically, they are dedicated to outlining some of the difficulties that affect that previous experience, which is forged during the accelerated development that culminates in the first birthday.

These chapters are like drawing back curtains and revealing various scenarios of life regarding babies of different ages. These scenarios illustrate, always from the perspective of the baby and the story of their experiences, various situations in which their signals are not picked up by their carers. *This is the guiding thread, different circumstances that hinder the establishment of communication.*

While reflecting on the stories, we can see the process which is involved for babies to engage and connect with "the world" during that first year of life. This is a very important process because the connection with this "world" will give them a reflection of who they are, and they can use this connection as a bridge to enter into the wider world.

In the chapter, 'Knock Knock, Is Anyone There?' the stories tell us what happens when the mother and father are present but cannot listen, their minds are elsewhere with concerns and worries.

In 'Information Flood! Give Me a Break, Please', we hear about what happens to children when their parents are not only present but too present. The carers cannot hear because they are not quiet enough to allow a two-way flow.

In the chapter 'I Miss You Where Are You?' the infants tell their experiences of mothers who are more or less physically present, but are actually very busy, or are even absent while on work trips. For this reason, they cannot be attentive to their children.

In the chapter 'I Can't Explain Myself Properly Yet: Even I Don't Understand Me', we see situations in which babies feel their mothers are present but are puzzled. They do not stop to interpret and they always respond to their children in the same way.

In 'There's a Lot of Noise There. Can You Hear Me?' the babies relate experiences involving parents who, even though are there to listen to them, they feel an "inner noise" that comes from a long way off. This noise interferes with infants' attempts to communicate with their caregivers.

In the chapter, 'Don't Push Me Too Much or Too Little… Just the Right Amount!' infants tell us how they feel and react when parents are not sensitive to their rhythms and the changes they experience. On a broader level, the baby's signals of change are muted by the parents' expectations.

Finally, the "Recapitulation" of *If Babies Could Talk* offers some reflections on the nature of the information given in these pages. What has been heard in the conversations of these babies and what has been elaborated from them, in the different chapters, is contextualised as part of scientific advances in the subject of early life known as the Science of Early Childhood Development.

I hope with all my heart that this book can help to give voice to babies and their world. I hope that it can offer to learn about one of the ages of life that is the most foundational because it constitutes our primal emotional territory: our childhood, our psychological homeland.

Thus, knowing more about the origins, we can help our children go out into the world better equipped and emotionally more secure. Our children have to inhabit the future to which they belong. We want that future to be a good place for them to live, in good company.

1
The Good Shadow of My Great Tree

A child takes their first steps without support, staggering and hesitant, usually towards us, who encourage them with open arms as a port to be reached. It is an event that marks a watershed for this human being. Without a doubt, it is a milestone in their motor development. In addition to this, it reproduces the moment when our ancestors, no longer needing their hands to support them in movement, freed them, to make those same hands bridges between our minds and the world: touching, handling, creating, building, embracing, caressing…

That may be the most visible thing about this moment, but something less obvious and yet absolutely fundamental also happens: this standing up is accompanied by the dawning of a self, the child's own self, which begins to be perceived strongly as being different from the one in front of them. *Actually, it is as if this standing up and getting going was not only something physical but also something psychological.*

All of a sudden, they begin to move as if there were no tomorrow, taking the world by storm. This is really daring for infants because to them everything is gigantic and there is plenty out there that might scare them. If a child knows who is there for them, they feel safe because they feel that there is someone stronger who, like a large tree, casts a shadow, a protective shield that accompanies them wherever they go. This security in that someone gives them the energy to put all their attention into exploring the world and exploring themselves within it.

Where does this security come from? It comes from a continuous experience with that person, from the moment the baby opens their eyes and sees themselves in the eyes of the other person, like a mirror. Little by little, they begin to recognise themselves in that image as someone valuable and loved. It is a bit like what happens to us as adults, why do you trust someone? It's because a person has repeatedly shown you that they are on your side, in good moments and bad ones; this becomes evident because they are predictable and consistent. They might get angry or not approve of something you do, to help you grow, but you know they are there for you unconditionally because they love you. They see, perhaps like no one else, how unique you are. This is what builds up within the most primary relationship; the one between the baby, totally vulnerable and lost, and their mother, or the adult who cares for them and protects them. That is why this is woven into the most intimate foundations of our being.

What happens when that adult, in the child's eyes, is not emotionally predictable? We can expect that this will generate a lot of confusion in the child's feelings and sense of security. *The big shady tree can become a little bush and the infant will feel that they cannot go on "adventures" into the world if there is no one standing behind them. If they are not sure of that someone, they cannot be sure of themselves or of who they are It will be more of a priority for the child to see what is happening with the bush.*

All this can be more terrifying and paralyzing for the infant than all the scares in the world, waiting out there. As a result, they will have fewer adventures and undertake less exploration than a friend who feels secure and safe. Moreover, they will have more doubts about themselves and others. Let us look at the following two stories told by Rose and Jack, both of whom have recently celebrated their first birthday. Rose and Jack talk with their respective friends.

A Daddy with Two Faces

Hi Rose! How are you today?

> Better, there has been a lot of trouble.

I'm glad you're feeling better because you've been telling me for a while that you've been sad and upset.

> Yes! Quite a lot actually. I've been having a bad time of it. I was really confused because my daddy sometimes looked at me with a lot of affection and at other times it was like he was not my daddy.

How strange, and your mummy did that too?

> No, because I heard that my mummy went to heaven and I don't see her. I see my aunt who is with us and my cousin.

Oh! But with your cousin, you have someone to play with?

> Not much. He's smaller than me. Anyway, at my age what happens is that we play close to each other, but each of us plays at something different. We haven't played together yet, although I think with time we will.

And what about your daddy?

> Well, sometimes I would be playing and he would come and hug me and then he would come back after a while and, I don't know, he would be different... like, he wouldn't smile at me the same way, or he would do something else, without paying much attention to me.

That's weird! What a mess.

> Thankfully, someone told my daddy that my emotions were getting messed up and I felt really insecure, that's why I was strange and uneasy. And when I felt bad or there was something that bothered me and I needed to get close to my father as a refuge... Well! That was the worst.

Because you didn't know what to do.

> Of course, I didn't know if I wanted to get close to my daddy to calm me down or get away from him, because I didn't really know how he was going to act with me. Then someone told my daddy that he had to grow a beard.

A beard! What does a beard have to do with all that?

> Because it turns out that my daddy has an identical brother, my Uncle! And we live together and of course, that's why everything seemed so strange to me. Now I have seen them together more, one with a beard who is my daddy, who is more handsome, and the other one is my uncle.

Ah! That's why sometimes your father approached you, and sometimes it was a double of your father, but really it was your uncle and you couldn't tell them apart. It was as if your father treated you in two different ways.

> You've got it. With the idea of the beard, now I know who my daddy is, and he always looks at me the same and I feel much safer and less upset inside. They also told my daddy that for me to have things clearer it would be good that, at least for a while, we spent

more time alone together, apart from the rest of the family.

Well, you're lucky they could advise your father.

You see, isn't life funny? We babies, are a world unto ourselves, eh!

What Luck! Mummy Works at a Nursery School

Are you attending school now, Jack?

Yes, I've been going for a few months now. But since I've been going, I've been very upset and very sad.

Do you cry?

A lot, just thinking about it makes me want to cry.

It'll pass. For a few days, I also got angry and didn't want Mummy to leave. But now I know that later she will come back, and the grown-ups are very affectionate. So I'm happier.

Well, my mummy leaves me in the morning, she gives me a lot of kisses and she encourages me a lot. But then, when I'm at school I see her enter my class, but she goes right past me and looks at me out of the corner of her eye.

But that's her coming to pick you up.

Noooo! She passes by like I say, and I look at her, all happy, and I raise my arms hoping she will pick me up. And nothing. She looks at me a little bit, passes, and leaves. I can't understand what has happened, she doesn't love me anymore...

Well, that's very strange... Tomorrow we'll talk some more. My daddy is taking me out of the highchair. Hopefully, I'm going to have a bath!

***

Hi again. I haven't heard from you for long. How was school today?

                                           Well, mystery solved!

Mystery? Tell me all about it!

> I heard my mother say that she was very happy and lucky to work at a nursery school because she could take me there and keep me close to her. But she also said that I was worrying her a lot because I looked sad, and sometimes angry, that I was sleeping badly and she couldn't understand what was wrong with me.

So, your mother doesn't drop you at the nursery school and come back later, when it is time to go home. She also works there!

> That's right, and I also heard her saying that she missed me so much that she used any excuse to come to my class to see me while she was working, even when she didn't have a proper reason. She spoke to someone who knows a lot about babies, because that person told her what was the reason I was sad and angry. Of course! How was I to know why my mummy was not picking me up when I was missing her so much? And this was happening several times a day...

Ahhh, of course, what a mess... poor Jack! But what now?

Well now, my mum says goodbye to me at the door of the class, and later when it is time to go, she picks me up, really delighted, and gives me lots of kisses and we go home. So I'm not looking at the door all the time in case she appears, and I'm calmer now that Mummy always behaves like Mummy!

It's a good solution. I'm glad. They are coming to take me to my dinner now... We'll talk soon!

Night night!

What Is Happening Here?

The children in the two stories are now a year old and, in different ways, are reporting similar experiences. They are very confused emotionally because for them the main figures in their lives behave inconsistently: sometimes they show they are emotionally connected to them and at other times they are more distant.

The experiences of these children, based on real cases, are unique and are almost like natural experiments which demonstrate everything that the science of babies has discovered in recent decades.

Rose lost her mother in a tragic accident when she was barely three months old. Her father is fortunate enough to have a generous and understanding brother who welcomes him into his own family, with his wife and son. There is an added peculiarity to this situation: the brothers are identical twins. Their job circumstances mean they are not often at home at the same time, so Rose doesn't see them together. Therefore, for Rose, there is only Daddy, and she does not know how this daddy is going to behave because actually the one who comes to her sometimes is not her father but her uncle. Obviously, her uncle has a different bond with her and that is transmitted emotionally. The father did not realise that his daughter was confusing them. He thought that people could distinguish him from his brother and he assumed that his daughter could do so because, curiously, he thought his voice was different from his brother's! He had not realised that he, like everyone else, heard his own voice from within and his brother's from outside. For those who were outside, their voices were practically identical.

The impact of the situation is important because at the end of the first year of life, Rose, like all children, begins to have expectations regarding the person who cares for and protects her. These expectations come from the experience of their relationship over the previous months: whether they have felt that person to be emotionally available, whether they connected in their interaction, whether that person's behaviour was predictable... If we put ourselves in their place, this gives us confidence in how the world "works", based on how we are doing in it, but it also gives us confidence in ourselves in relation to that world: we are "someone" with whom others can connect because we are loved and protected. If we have the experience, repeated in multiple ways, of going to the one who takes care of us and that adult protects us and welcomes us emotionally, then, when something disturbs or scares us or we have just fallen, we run towards that person for comfort and they provide it. Thus, with a renewed spirit, we can return to what we really want; to explore, experiment and learn.

But things for Rose are different. Her expectations are based on the relationship with a person that for her has two faces, emotionally speaking, and that makes him unpredictable. Therefore, when Rose is anxious and needs to calm down, on one hand she needs to get close and look for the contact that comforts her but, on the other hand, she is not sure how he will react; this means she has to rely on her own, still scarce, resources to regulate her emotions, which are very intense. She explains to her friend, in her own way, her disorientation, which becomes visible in situations that stress her and in which these expectations are activated in the search for that secure base. If the expectations come from a relationship that is, in her experience, unreliable when they are activated, then poor Rose breaks down. *If this is not remedied, it will have negative repercussions on her emotional and behavioural development, including problems relating with other children but also with adults.*

We might think that Rose's story is exceptional, but from her point of view, the experience is with one person who is not emotionally predictable for her. That is why the story of Jack deals with much the same thing, although in this case, it is really the same person.

In Jack's family, everyone is very happy because when Jack's mother goes back to work, she will not have to face that temporary separation of having to leave Jack with somebody. Jack's mother works at a nursery school. However, when you put yourself in Jack's place, this situation can be traumatic. He arrives at "school" with Mummy, entering into a situation of being with other children and with a stranger who attends to them all, and then, much to his bewilderment, he sees Mummy! What his body asks for is to embrace her, and for her to take him away, or at least to assure him that everything is fine, to see if it gives him the courage to try again with all the new things around him. However, Mummy is not the one who is looking after that group of children and she is just pretending to need something in order to keep an eye on him; because she misses him so much, she just wants to see how he is. Because of her role in this situation, she cannot behave as a mother but must behave like one of the staff at the nursery school.

Let us go back to that healthy exercise of putting ourselves in their place or, better yet, transferring that situation to our adult life. The person you love suddenly goes past, and it is like they know you, but not as much as at other times. The next time you saw that person, you would have many doubts about how to act and you would be angry; and this is what happens to us, who are adults and have a sophisticated mind and complex language…

Jack is like Rose and all children aged just over a year: they are building their minds and, above all, organising themselves emotionally. They say, who am I in relation to the other, to the world? This is developed precisely based on this inter-subjective space between them and the person who cares for and protects them.

These situations can also occur when the mother has a small local business: a hairdresser, a shop... The child is in sight, perhaps in a playpen, but when there are more costumers and work the mother cannot respond to the child, and from the child's perspective this can produce some of the feelings and confusion that Rose and Jack told us about.

What These Stories Teach Us

These stories teach us *the importance of being in harmony in the relationship between the figure of reference, the primary caregiver, and the baby.* They teach us the importance of coherence throughout the first year of life so that, when the infant starts to get an idea of who they are and how it works "out there", they feel safe.

They also teach us that situations which seem at first glance to be beneficial, such as having a generous brother in difficult times, or a mother working in a nursery school, may not be so positive. They can cause important problems for babies in a way that for their parents are incomprehensible simply because of a lack of knowledge of the development processes of a baby's mind. When we understand the bases of these processes, we can reorient our actions to facilitate healthy emotional development.

In fact, communication with the baby, in order to be effective and achieve that harmony, requires that we can develop a presence that is physically and emotionally attentive. In addition, we must be in charge of the situation so that we encourage their autonomy and guide them towards it. In the following chapters, we are going to see different situations in which the development of this attunement suffers when listening is not working. The child does not feel that their signals and clues are responded to attentively from the "other side" and they share those experiences with other babies in their lively chats.

2
Knock Knock, Is Anyone There?

When a human being opens their eyes to this world for the first time, they do not see much, they do not yet distinguish forms and have very little control over what they focus on. Then everything is activated and the changes begin.

The need to communicate with another human being is vital. This communication is initially established at very basic levels, more in line with the most active structures of the brain: smell, touch, contact, vibrations. However, that is just the beginning of a phenomenal display of levels and subtleties that babies develop through their connection with those adults whom they need for their physical and emotional survival.

In the first six months, when they cannot move around, they need the world to come to them and they develop all kinds of signals to get our attention. *They do not always know what is happening to them and for that they also need us, to see if we can figure out something to make them feel a little better.*

In the daily routine and from moment to moment, when they have us in front of them, they communicate in their own way. They send us their signals. Since often these signals are not clear to us, we need to have a clear mind. Indeed, for the signals to arrive, there needs to be a space in our minds, a certain attention and interest. Therefore, when the signals arrive and we talk to the babies interpreting what happens to them, or we just look at them and touch them, or we figure out that maybe they are hungry or uncomfortable, we are giving them references to what they feel inside. This constitutes the scaffolding upon which they can organise themselves and install more "floors" in their emerging minds.

The connection is generated by responding to all their needs, including their need for affection, in a timely and appropriate manner with emotional availability. Thus, the child perceives that the "other" (representative of the world) is predictable and can be trusted.

However, life is complicated and it takes its own course. Sometimes we go through painful situations. When there is a lot of noise, many waves and personal disorientation, the curtains of our senses shut and only some light passes through. This makes it very difficult to take care of our baby at the level that their mind requires.

What is more, because of their enormous fragility, babies are wonderfully equipped to detect subtle changes in our mood and emotions. It is not that they understand the matter fully, of course, but their radar tells them "danger – there is no connection". It is like when we are talking to someone and their eyes indicate a change which tells us that they are not with us because their mind has taken them somewhere else. If this is an occasional distraction between adults, it doesn't matter. If there is a relationship of trust, we might click our fingers and say: "Hey, come back, I'm talking to you!" But if this situation happens with a baby and persists over time, then the baby perceives that something is wrong and, being unable to click their fingers, they will most likely switch off, or cry more, or be more tense and irritable. Of course, for them, there is a danger because the other person is not mindfully present. If that person is not there, who will the infant hold onto, who will they tune in with, to keep making sense of this complex world and of themselves within it?

Let us open our ears and our hearts to listen to the stories that Jerome, Sophie and Mark are going to tell us. The children speaking are all within their first year of life. Jerome is eight months old, Sophie is aged four months and Mark six months. They talk with their respective friends.

Mummy Is Not Responding

Hi Jerome, yesterday we couldn't talk but you were looking worried.

> Yes. Because my mummy used to sing to me but for a while, she has had red eyes and sometimes when she thinks I am asleep in her arms, I feel her crying. When she is like that, it is like she is in her own mind and I have to cry loudly or scream for her to "come back".

Hmmm. But is your mum alone with you?

> Not at all. Everyone at home is really worked up and they carry me from place to place…

So, more movement, more fun, right?

> It's not as good as it sounds. I like my routines and with so much picking up and putting down, each person treats me in a different way. That irritates me a lot. Then, I cry and then things get worse and more upsetting!

You'll have to tough it out.

> At my age, I'm still learning to handle everything happening outside along with what is going on inside. My system gets overloaded!

Well, I don't know what to say… and why is there so much trouble in your house?

> My granddad has come to live at home and, like me, spends a lot of time in bed. They have put this really strange baby bottle, like tubes, into his mouth. And my mother kisses him and caresses him.

Phew! I wouldn't like that bottle, one you can't suck and play with.

> Me neither, I prefer mine. I've heard the grown-ups saying that my granddad was very ill. I don't know what they mean... maybe his tummy hurts, like mine does sometimes.

If his tummy is sore, it must be serious, because when ours hurt it's the worst!

> People tell my mummy that she needs a helping hand. My daddy gives her a lot of hugs.

Well, it seems you have a problem at home.

> Yes, it seems so. But someone is helping my mum to organise the new situation a bit so that, when she is with me, she can enjoy my wonderful company.

How modest of you, Jerome!

> But it's true. I can do faces, and make anyone who is in front of me laugh! But of course, I have to feel confident and know that the other person is with me, not just in body, but paying full attention too. I pick up immediately if they are thinking of other things, or they are smiling with sad eyes.

I know what you mean, it happens to me too. It's horrible when you don't know what to make of it, especially when they smile at you but their eyes are cold or sad. When the smile isn't convincing, it looks like a grimace... A next-door neighbour always does that to me when I go out in my buggy, and I start pouting so that my mum takes me away from her.

> It happens to me with a cousin who visits us from time to time.

And what about your mum. Has she got any better?

> It looks like it has. Mummy and I were together for a while this afternoon and we had a great time. We played peek-a-boo and, when I saw that my mummy was there just for me, I turned on the charm and played everything in my repertoire.

I hope it lasts. Your mum has lots of things to worry about. Now I'm off, I'm going to see if Daddy wants to play with me.

My Mum Is So Pretty

Hey, Sophie, why the sad face?

> It's my mummy, she is really pretty but she looks like a picture, she doesn't smile. I think I'm starting to look like her.

Well, if you were as pretty as her that would be good, but as for not smiling that's not so good…

> What do you mean?

Because when we come into this world, since we can't go looking for anything, we have to make the world come to us. And the first thing is to cry good and strong, but soon we have to learn to smile so that people stay with us. So learning to smile is basic, My girl!

> Ah… my mum and I are alone all the time, and some nights a little while before I go to sleep, I see my daddy.

Don't you have grandparents and cousins?

> No. Because my mum is not from here, she is from far away and my daddy is older and I think he doesn't have another family.

Hmmm… So I reckon that your mum feels lonely, and that's why she isn't smiling. And because you are so little and you're with her all the time, if she doesn't smile then you won't either.

> Well, I'm going now because I think today I'll be lucky and we'll go for a walk for a while. Here is Mummy coming to put me into the buggy.

Great! See you later!

> See you!

***

Hi there, Sophie! I haven't had news of you for days. Today, you look happier.

> Yes, my mummy was talking to someone who told her to speak to me in her beautiful language and now she talks more to me. It's even like her voice sounds more familiar to me now.

Sure. Probably you recognise it from hearing her speak in her own language when you were in her tummy and started to hear things.

> That's probably what it is. I had no idea! She has also been told to do things that she likes and that makes her feel good, like using a screen to chat with her family and friends in her homeland. Now, for an hour in the afternoon we go to a place that I heard is free

to use for speaking and when we leave, she is smiling, and I copy her! And I am seeing my dad more as well.

Wow! Anything else?

Yeah! There is more. She has also started an English class and she has met people there. She takes me in the buggy and when we are on the way back home, she talks to me and smiles at me. We are much happier!

I'm really glad for you. For sure, mums who are on their own or who feel lonely don't feel right at all. And neither do we.

It's true! I'll see you another day because she is coming, all happy, to take me for a bath.

Very Noisy Mum and Dad

Oh, I'm really confused.

Yes, Mark, and you also cry a lot because I saw you in the park.

It's all very strange. My parents speak very loudly and when I look at their faces, they are all red, just like when I cry because something hurts and I don't know what it is. Well, like that, but without the crying.

That sounds like an argument.

It could be, but sometimes there is a lot of noise and sometimes it is all very quiet.

And when there is more racket, what do you do?

I cry hard. I'm afraid.

And does that help?

> No. Well, I don't know. Sometimes they get angry and shout more and say my name.

Yeah. Sometimes grown-ups have complicated lives.

> Well, ours are too!

Yes, it's true, and there are loads of things that they don't know about us.

> Now, it seems we are going to another house.

Forever?

> I don't know. I think just my mum and I are going, and we'll live with Granny.

And is your dad going, too?

> I don't know, I haven't seen him for days.

Maybe he had to go on a trip for work.

> I suppose so. But I miss him. Besides, he didn't say goodbye to me.

Probably you were asleep.

> Maybe... but then I would have liked not to be asleep.

Well, I'll let you go now because they are coming to take me to eat dinner and I'm starving.

> OK, enjoy your dinner!

What Is Happening Here?

The three children in these stories, Jerome, Sophie and Mark, tell us in their own way about the disorientation that they feel when they do not experience a direct connection with their carers and how this sometimes makes them raise the volume of their signals in the hope that this time their parent will respond. At other times, what they experience is a great uneasiness and restlessness that makes them cry at a bad time, as in the case of the noisy parents.

For Jerome, at eight months, not only is it disturbing to see his mother emotionally more absent, but this also affects his routines that are so important to him right now. Moreover, as it has been a few weeks since his memory began to emerge, he is at a stage during which he expresses his discomfort to people with whom he is not familiar, and now the house is full of "strange" people. That is why, when his friend tells him that he will have to put up with it, poor Jerome replies: 'At my age, I'm still learning to handle everything happening outside along with what is going on inside. My system gets overloaded!' His radar is also becoming more sensitive to "false smiles". Along with that, he also begins to be a little more aware of the impact he has on others, especially when he does "tricks", as he says. Now, Jerome gets so much fun out of playing peek-a-boo with his mum because of his increased awareness that even if he cannot see his mother she is still there.

Sophie, a four-month-old, is chatting with her friend who is a little older, because from what Sophie says he realises that Sophie's mother feels very lonely. At Sophie's age, a baby who spends all the time with a mother in these conditions will show their mother's mood in their facial expression, like a mirror. When she says that her mum is happier, she also tells us that she herself smiles more.

With his noisy parents, Mark, aged six months, is very worried when he sees the adults with red faces, shouting. He absorbs the tone of their emotions and when he cries, scared, this increases the stress in the situation. At this time, he is beginning to have an incipient memory, which is why he says that he has not seen his father for days and the friend tells him that maybe he was asleep when he left. Mark replies that he would have liked his father to have said goodbye because if not, it is as if his father has disappeared.

In short, they are telling us about feelings of irritation and emotional confusion, like Jerome, or reflecting the lack of expressiveness of a depressed mother, like Sophie, or just being scared, like Mark. If these situations persist, they will undoubtedly affect the emotional development of the three infants. By continually having the experience that their signals stumble against a kind of invisible wall that does not allow them to reach the other person, their sense of security that is built on the connection will be negatively affected.

These stories tell about complicated lives in the midst of raising a baby. However, these situations occur very frequently because they are part of life. The grandfather who becomes seriously ill and has to be looked after at home; the woman who comes from another country and another culture who feels terribly isolated; and the couple who have serious problems with living together who may be in the process of breaking up. All have one thing in common: these are highly stressful situations.

Knowing that a loved one is very sick, for example, one of our own parents, naturally makes us sad. Along with the fact that our emotions are affected, the situation demands attention on various fronts that include our time and dedication to attend to them or to organise others to take care of them. In addition, it is often an initial process of crisis that can later result in the sick person moving to live in our home during a temporary convalescence, or even permanently. This is the situation that is illustrated in the first case. Naturally, if at the same time, a baby is being raised then the carer will often act routinely, almost on automatic pilot, because their emotions and their own physical capacity are overloaded.

Living in a culture that is alien to us and at the same time raising a child can become a very difficult experience to cope with, because of the feelings of being uprooted, missing everything that is familiar to us, and the loneliness this brings.

The second case presents the outline of a situation like that, in which, although the mother makes an effort, the difficulty of the experience is too much for her and affects her emotionally. This mother feels too sad and alone to enjoy Sophie. Her life has taken a huge turn and she has yet to come to terms with it, personally speaking, and adapt to everything involved in being in a new country. Being so isolated does not help and little Sophie, although she can be a company for her mother, can only really be a passive witness to the situation.

If a romantic relationship goes through ups and downs, or it breaks up completely, the process is especially difficult in the postnatal period. There are latent conflicts that, when a child arrives, come out into the open. Sometimes, complications occur during the pregnancy and then the first months with the baby will be especially tiring, in physical and psychological terms. The impact of that on the couple's relationship has not been foreseen and so it suffers. In this context, the father has difficulty finding his place and, on top of that, fatherhood brings its own changes that he will have to process.

It can happen, in other situations, that when activating all those feelings and desires about what to do with a child, the parents realise that they are very different. Maybe because they have never spoken about this before or if they have, reality confronts them with day-to-day situations for which they are not very well equipped.

Whether for one, or several, of these possibilities, a conflict is unleashed. Being tired does not help. In all of this, Mark has a hard time at a stage that is particularly sensitive for his own emotional development.

Children are easily frightened, this is natural, and rightly so since they are such little things in a big, confusing world. Research has shown that if they are exposed to high levels of stress continuously, their brain structures, which are expanding rapidly, are affected. They become hypervigilant to what surrounds them, and also very anxious.

The mothers in these stories are going through stressful situations. These external stressors, when they occur, take up all our attention but, above all, drain our emotional energy and cause us wear and tear that at times can be overwhelming.

The common denominator of these stories is that life situations of this kind affect a person emotionally. The person in question here is the caregiver who is so important for the baby because they constitute the primary reference. Thus, the person is sadder, but also more absent and lost in her own thoughts, trying to find some direction in troubled and stormy waters.

If we transfer this to other spheres of life, for example, work, and we think of these people in such situations at their workplace, what would we expect? It is very likely that they would make mistakes due to distraction and that they would feel tired and not attend to their tasks properly. In addition, this would get worse, the more difficult the task and the more attention or diligence this required. Caring for a baby can be considered a very difficult task because children send their caregivers signals of need that are not always clear even to the infants themselves. Therefore, in that context, it is very easy to make many mistakes and enter into a dynamic of confusion with the baby that either intensifies their calls or means that the infant becomes passive and gives up, as happens in cases where the mother is clearly depressed.

What These Stories Teach Us?

These stories teach us the importance of knowing what babies need emotionally at that stage. *We should not naively believe that they do not know or understand anything.* They learn in their own way, one that is essentially emotional, and they express this through irritability, mood swings, in their sleep patterns and in their appetite. Their repertoire is very limited.

All this means that if we are ever in a situation of stress, like one of those recounted here by our little friends, or something similar, we need to be aware of the impact on the baby. Therefore, we should ask for help in order to find a way to lessen that impact as much as possible; it might be from friends or relatives, or it can be a professional help. Some stressors that we suffer, we cannot change. However, we can create a kind of "firewall" so we can keep some space free of smoke in order to be with our baby. Doing this will contribute greatly to the emotional well-being of the baby and, ultimately, to that of the whole family.

3
Information Flood! Give Me a Break, Please

Our children's arrival in this life is, for them, almost like landing on a foreign planet. Absolutely everything is new. They have to adapt to everything that exist and is happening, not only around them, but also within their changing bodies. For this adaptation, they rely on their multiple windows onto the world, which gradually matures with use, and also on the parental embraces that contain them so that they do not come apart completely in the midst of so much chaos.

If we look around, at that table there, or the floor, or that wall, we will realise that we have a certain sensory knowledge of all these things: something is hard or soft, rough or smooth, it does not bend, or maybe it does, it smells… it tastes like plastic. For newborns, all these are elements of information to be incorporated into their minds. However, for such a huge task they do not have many resources. It will take a few months until they can reach out to them, bring them to their mouths, experience them, that is, be physically more proactive.

This is about the basics. Yet the same happens, although in a more complex way, with the things that occur around them: movement, people and also emotions both outside and inside them. That is why the information that reaches their brains, all of which is new, is like a tsunami, one that is almost continuous. Their little brains have to work ceaselessly, at the rate of a million new interconnections of neurons per second.

It is not surprising that they have to sleep to shut down and reset their system before it becomes blocked completely and their irritation and discomfort become unbearable.

Experiences they have in their relationship with the person who takes care of them, *when they are in tune with them*, have the important function of cushioning the restlessness produced by the enormous daily task of processing everything that comes to them.

When babies connect with the adult and this person calms them down, and they link into a rhythm they can withstand, one that is neither too fast nor too slow, then their stress is lowered to a tolerable level, their mind is activated but not overwhelmed. Thus, their mind is at the optimum level to process what surrounds them and gradually becomes able to absorb more and more.

Often, as parents, we are so excited about our long-awaited offspring that we are in a hurry to give them everything we have been dreaming of since before they arrived. We are excited to see their progress and, sometimes, we see advances where there are none and we press on even more. However, without realising it we are imposing our agenda on them, believing that we are simply encouraging them to move ahead.

Actually, in these cases, our minds are ultra-focussed on our child, and our thoughts are not elsewhere or full of worries, as in the case of parents who are stressed for other reasons. However, the result is nonetheless also a short circuit in communication, although for very different reasons. It is like a conversation in which, if there is no place for you to have a say, the result is a monologue. This is the kind of situation in which someone may spend perhaps half an hour talking to themselves through you!

Much to our regret, and with all our efforts, the results may not be as expected. These children do not find the necessary resonance of their signals in the adult who is very busy giving and explaining. *They do not connect because they are not given a turn to express themselves and so the emotional dialogue that is needed badly remains unformed.*

Beth and Michel, with their stories, illustrate experiences of this kind while they talk with their respective friends. Beth is about three months old and Michel is a little older, around eleven months.

My Mum and Dad Take Extra Care of Me

Hello Beth! You don't look so good.

> You're dead right. My parents are overwhelming me!

Overwhelming you... how?

> All I have to do is open my eyes and they are on me with toys, asking me for a smile. At my age, I need some space!

Space... and for them to go sloooowly.

> Yes, yes, that's it. I need them to go slowly and to give me space. Of course, as they are so happy with me, they can't contain themselves, the poor things.

I know exactly what you mean. If they knew more about how our little brains and our rhythms work...

> Right, and we would all have a better time of it. Can you believe that when they are with me and I turn my head to look away, just to have a break, they follow me with the rattle because they think I'm not interested in things!

I see. Of course, not speaking their language yet has its problems. Well, my parents are with me almost all the time, but I never get overloaded.

> I suppose that way you play more happily, at your own pace.

It's not that, my parents spend a lot of time looking at their hands and sometimes they smile at their hand. Other times, they speak to their hand and smile at it…

> At their hand? How's that?

Well, they are holding me and they have something in their other hand. And they move their thumb and things must be happening there because they smile or move their heads… I look at them and I only see Mummy's ear and hair, what they call the "profile"… At other times it's like the thing is surrounded by Mummy's hair, it's quite strange. I would love to be like that thing so that they look at me.

> I think I heard that this thing you are talking about is called a "mobile".

A mobile? Well, it's not very mobile because it doesn't move from their hands. And with all the things, I have yet to discover and find out about this world… What I do is yawn and protest and sometimes, with a bit of luck, they look at me. Crying works quite well too.

> Maybe, they can give you a mobile too.

But what I need is to feel, suck, bite, smell and feel everywhere. Can you do that with a mobile? I've already sucked it once and they didn't like it at all. The two of them together told me: 'No, not in your mouth!' And they took it from me. I don't understand what it's good for.

It's like a window through which things happen. Later on, you get good in passing your finger from one side to another, there's a lot of colour and noise… I've seen it because they put every single thing in front of my eyes.

But. can you get hold of these things you see so that you can play with them?

I don't think so. The things are inside the box, and my little hands aren't good at handling things yet…

That sounds really boring! Well, I'll let you go because my mommy looks like she's coming to pick me up and I'm going to make the most of the moment as she has nothing in her hands.

OK, here comes my mum for me too, with two toys, one in each hand! Oh no!

Good luck Beth, What about pretending to be asleep?

Mummy and Daddy Want the Very Best for Me

Hi Michel, how are things going?

Well, I don't know. Now that I've passed the babbling phase in Code for Communicating with Grown-ups (CCG), and I'm just starting with words, I have this complete jam.

Yeah, I already know how to say two things in CCG: "Mummy" and "No".

Yes, it's about time for that, and I understand some things but it's like a traffic jam in there. I don't know

> how to put my tongue for all those sounds, or what goes with what. I tell you, I don't know whether I'm coming or going!

Probably you can manage it by pointing with your finger and say "hmm hmm", and your mum or your dad gives you what you want. Yeah, you lazy lump!

> Well, you're wrong there, you know it all, my mum is French, and my dad is from here.

Really, what a bit of luck! Your mother will speak to you in French and your father in English because those are their native languages, their "mother tongues", and those are the ones they should use to communicate with you.

> Well, that's all true, and although it is a bit difficult. I am managing more or less.

So?

> Well, my mum and dad want me to have a great education because they want me to be very intelligent, and that is why they want me to learn many languages from a young age.

What do you mean? I'm getting confused.

> Well, they take me to a nursery where everyone speaks to me in another language, in something different. And then in between, they give us a session with songs and games in a language that is not the same as before… I heard that it is Mandarin Chinese, which will be very useful for the future.

But my boy, we haven't even blown out the candle on our first birthday!

> Yeah, exactly. Imagine!

You are trying to say your first words and there are four CCGs out there! Poor guy, I'm not surprised you have a traffic jam.

> They are so interested in me and they are so happy that they don't skimp on things to give me all the opportunities. I heard them telling someone that this way, from the very start I am on the road to univer…something.

Well, my friend, it would be good for you if they let time take its course. Even if they have big dreams for you, what you need right now comes first.

> Yes, because if I can speak a CCG in two versions with my lovely mummy and with my dad, when I am older I will be more ready to take on another CCG.

Of course, it will be a bit more difficult for you than for me, because everyone speaks to me in one language, but in your case, since it's your mum and dad it is worth making that extra effort. But with that big mixture of CCGs, even if you do manage to get there eventually, the delays might be too much for you.

> And I don't see the need right now, when I am just starting to put the first CCG into my head.

As my mum says, "one comes before two", meaning, take things step by step, and make sure the base is firm before starting to build.

> I'm off now. It looks like they are coming to take me off to the big muddle. I can already feel a knot starting in my head and on my tongue!

Well, Good luck!

What Is Happening Here?

In these stories, little Beth is talking to a four-month-old friend. Michel is with another baby of the same age and both are nearly a year old.

Our two protagonists are saturated with information. There is no space for them to express or even process and digest everything that comes at them.

The speed, quantity and difficulty are well above the level of operation of their systems, so to speak. What they are receiving does not propel them forward, but rather adds weights to their wings, making it more difficult for them to fly upwards.

Beth has dedicated parents who have read everything in sight about parenting. They can hardly wait for her to wake up to show her all kinds of toys, talk to her, touch her… They celebrate every tiny gesture the girl makes, even if it is out of fatigue because in their enthusiasm they confuse this with smiles that encourage them for more. Sometimes they compete among themselves to see who does more. There is no place for her to experience and absorb things at her own pace within the emotional "embrace" provided by her mother or father. This way of communicating with Beth, if it persists, will affect her emotional development because it is stifling her initiative and is probably pushing her to concentrate more on objects rather than on people in order to gain a little space and control in the midst of so much stimulation.

It is paradoxical because parents stimulate their children thinking that they will respond at the same level. However, often they comment with some perplexity that as the months pass the child "ignores us", "is very independent" or "they do their own thing", without seeing that their child has been trying to adapt as well as they can to the situation that they find themselves in.

In order to respond appropriately, we need some calm to observe and know what the other is saying. This is a very serene listening in which we devote ourselves to feeling the response that arises in us based on what we receive. We need that attitude of getting to know our baby. In the story, Beth's friend mentions two key things an infant needs, giving the child space and keeping their pace.

Space and pace are really the coordinates of the face-to-face relationship with the baby. We have to give the infants their space. For example, that rattle that is shaken a centimetre from their face is inside their space. Therefore, if we do this, it is because we are starting a certain game but we go little by little to see whether it pleases the child. So, we wait and if they respond with excitement and joy, we keep going; but, because we are aware we are inside their space, at the first sign of displeasure or fatigue we stop doing this. In terms of time, we have to go slowly because we need to go at their pace, not ours. They are the ones that are growing into the world. Therefore, they set the rhythm and, like with dance, once we have joined with that rhythm we can maybe make it go a little faster, but always taking care that the child does not switch off or show signs that it is too much.

Michel's story also illustrates, like Beth's, the experience of an avalanche of information that requires a capacity for management that he does not yet have and that, in fact, hinders him from absorbing it in his own time.

The development of language is a great milestone for the child because it is an instrument of the greatest importance and one with which the development of his thought is intertwined. Together, language and thought become for children their "seven-league boots". Those magic boots which they can use to travel the world in great strides and recreate it within their own universe of meanings and emotions.

It does not matter in which language this master key is acquired. What is important is that it does not take too long, because other advances depend on this. The expression "mother tongue" is used because it is the first one learned. These are the words, the sounds and their melody that we hear, muffled by water, and mixed with so many rhythms and pulses, in our mother's womb. When the circumstance occurs, as happens with Michel, that his parents have two different languages, the appropriate thing is that each one addresses the baby in their own language, not so much so that the infant learn more, but because feelings and emotions throb at the heart of our mother tongue. The emotional connection between the child and the carer is facilitated if the adult uses the verbal codes of their "affectionate mode". This is Michel's reality, he is growing up and coexisting with two adults who love him and transmit this to him in different verbal codes. The crucial thing is for him to connect with them, and once this foundation is settled, from there, further advancement can take place.

From the perspective of Beth and Michel, what their stories have in common, when we think about relationships and communication, is the hyper-presence of their mothers and fathers. In contrast with those parents who are physically present but whose problems do not allow them to be fully emotionally available, these parents are there in body and soul. However, despite the apparent difference, the emotional connection and communication also suffer. Beth is overwhelmed, she cries and becomes irritable with tiredness without being able to open a gap, space or pause that allows her to go at an acceptable rhythm, one that lets her experience things by participating.

Michel, somewhat older, also experiences his mother and father as over-present. At this stage, this manifests itself in the diversity of languages to which he is exposed. This can overwhelm him and hamper his progress in understanding and producing language. Michel starts from an advantageous situation because he has two languages at home. Therefore, he will learn both languages spontaneously, although, at the beginning, the pace of this learning may or may not slow down a little. It is about consolidating his skills in these two languages, giving them time and practice.

There is time for Michel to take advantage of the opportunities that his parents wish to give him. There are advantages to learning a language early, but many people have learned a language later in life and are perfectly competent in it. In general, if you aspire not only to learn a language but also to express yourself, without an accent, like a native speaker, it is advisable to do so before ten years of age. However, there are many people who, learning a language at a later age, have also managed to speak with total competence and without an accent. *What this means is that you do not have to be in a hurry and that the emotional well-being of the baby must come first.* A girl or boy who has a healthy emotional development, including a consolidated linguistic capacity for communication, is very well equipped to learn other languages.

What These Stories Teach Us?

These stories teach us how important it is to listen, in the broad sense of the word, but also to listen to the silences, to those pauses that shape language. Like with those old radio sets, we must tune in our receivers, listening out for the broadcasting signal. This can only be done if we keep quiet and pay attention. *There is listening at this immediate "face-to-face" level, but also listening on a broader level.* On this more general level we have to be well aware of what the other needs, so as to avoid situations in which we are giving, but not having paid enough attention, we end up giving what is not needed or was not asked for.

4
I Miss You, Where Are You?

When they are born, human beings arrive in the lives of their parents and into their specific circumstances. They might be the first child or the second. They arrive into the life of a young, or not so young, couple, who might have been together for a long time or just a short while. They might be the first child for the mother, but not for the father, who may have other children from previous relationships. They may arrive in a home where there is only a mother. Whatever the situation, they arrive into the particular circumstances, of life and of work, that the mother and/or father are experiencing at that moment.

In this context, needs to fit in with each other but the adults will have to do more adapting than the children, since babies have more urgent needs. Life, in its eagerness to get ahead, presses hard on the accelerator in the early years. In just 36 months, or three years, that baby which weighs just a few kilos at birth, and who has barely begun to use air to breathe, turns into a little person before our eyes. In those 36 months, the first twelve go at twice the speed of the subsequent ones.

By the age of three, our baby has become a little person who tells us things that have happened to them, imitates our activities, runs and jumps, draws and scribbles and can eat and go to the bathroom independently. This child interacts with friends and family, asks about everything, understands the rules and follows them, mostly, and is a learning machine whose curiosity and enthusiasm surprises us every day.

They do not, and cannot, travel that extraordinary journey alone. Children need our attentive presence and our emotional shelter in order to incorporate themselves into the world. They need this in a more particular and continuous way at the beginning. They need our eyes to return incipient sensations of self-perception. Therefore, they are constantly issuing signals to bring the world to them, since they cannot yet go out to it, and to retain and reflect on it when they have it at their fingertips.

On this journey, an hour or a day is a long time because many things happen on the scale of times and changes in which they move. What is more, their waking time is quite short since their activity is very intense and they need to reset their brains by sleeping a generous number of hours. We are talking about, on average, four or five hours awake each day in the first two months, nine hours per day by the age of a year, and twelve hours per day at the age of three. Therefore, their progress and all these dizzying changes occur with the information and experience that they accumulate in those few hours of daily wakefulness.

The personal situation of the mothers, after the first few postnatal months, may lead them to resume work. Often during the last months of the pregnancy, especially if there have been complications, the mother stops working. These circumstances make the work accumulate, particularly if they are self-employed, they are part of a small business or they work from home. Mothers, then, are dragged away to their business affairs at all hours, generally with a mobile, tablet or computer.

This results in situations in which the baby is by our side, even in our arms, but we continue our multitasking. The baby can look at us and even send us their signals, but as far as they are concerned, we are absent, an occupied presence and therefore an absent one. In this case, the absence is not due to being worried or sad, which also implies an "absent presence", as we saw in the previous chapter. It is due to the fact that we are literally doing something else such as answering a message or taking a phone call. At other times, because of fatigue, the father or mother may have the infant awake by their side or in their arms, and be watching TV. At the end of the day, it is the same situation: there is no "dialogue" because that takes two.

There are also jobs that require the caregiver to travel frequently, and with different schedules. Undoubtedly, this extra difficulty adds tension and stress to daily life because that person is still recovering and adapting to all the changes. *For the baby, additional organisation is needed in these cases since such comings and goings can be quite confusing.*

The experiences that Paul, Beth's interlocutor in the previous chapter, and Teresa discuss with their respective friends illustrate these situations. Paul is four months old and Teresa eight months.

Mummy Smartphonehands

How are you doing Paul?

> Oh! I don't know, I feel weak, and sometimes I get irritated.

What's wrong?

> A few days ago, I told our friend Beth that my mum is with me but she is always doing something, even when she has me in her arms.

But mums are always busy, Paul!

> I suppose so... since I don't have another mum, I don't know, I only know mine. And my dad, too. Sometimes my mum and dad prop me up between them on the sofa with some cushions, and I spend my time looking from one side to the other, just seeing ears.

Ears?

> Yes, because they are with what Beth told me is called a mobile, although I have also seen something a little bigger, a screen with things on it. Each of the two has their own device. So, that's why I look right and left and all I can see is just ears.

That doesn't sound good!

> When I get tired and protest, they look at me. So, I complain more and more to get them to pay attention to me.

That's something, I suppose.

> Yes, but they look at me with concern, trying to get me to be quiet, and they give me a toy mobile, and as soon as I close my mouth they go back to their mobiles.

Wow!

> I would like so much to spend some time every day watching my mum's face talking to me and whispering things, or being with Dad making faces. You learn a lot and it makes you laugh.

But you must have other times of the day when you eat for example, that is a good opportunity.

Other times?

Yeah! I have just started with baby food, but I also have breakfast and dinner with Mummy's milk, which sometimes goes into the bottle and Daddy gives it to me. I like those little moments a lot because we look at each other and they touch my face and they say sweet things to me and I give them my best smiles and I say in their code "dadadada" or "bababa".

And they don't have their mobiles in the other hand, taking advantage of the fact that you are sucking?

Hardly at all...

You're lucky your mum and dad aren't as busy as mine.

Grown-ups lives are complicated and they have to work hard for us too.

That's right, I've heard that mine work from home...

That's the worst because if the work is at home, everything is mixed up all the time.

I'm off now. Mummy is coming to give me some milk before going to bed, and luckily I think she is coming with empty hands!

See you some other time. Make the most of it!

Mummy and Her Seat-less Pram

Teresa, you look great in that lovely dress!

Yes, Mummy brought it for me as a present from her trip.

Has she been travelling?

Yes, she does it a lot. In the hall at home, we have my pram and her suitcase, which looks like a pram with wheels but without a seat. My mum takes her suitcase and then after a few days and nights she is home again.

And who is with you?

> My dad sometimes, but the ones I am with most are Jenny, who comes to take care of me, and with my grandma, who also comes.

Well, that's OK, isn't it?

> Well, not really… because I'm really anxious and I don't sleep at all well, and I'm very restless. Sometimes I fall asleep and I see my mummy's face saying good night and then I wake up and she is gone. If I close my eyes, she goes away! And I don't see her again for ages.

Phew! That's scary!

> Yeah, isn't it? I never know what's going to happen to her. I also see Daddy sometimes and sometimes not, and as soon as I'm distracted, he disappears too.

Well, I'll leave you for now. Let's hope things get better.

> See you later, I'll let you know. I'm going to be on the alert so that they don't leave me.

***

I haven't seen you for ages, Teresa!

> Yes, it's true. Where have you been?

We went on holiday and we were with my grandma and grandpa and my cousins. How are you?

> I have been going to nursery school for a few weeks.

What a bit of news! How is that, though? I thought
you told me your parents wanted you to be at home
for longer.

> My parents were worried because I was sleeping
> badly and eating worse. Since we spoke, I started
> feeling even odder. Also, I suddenly started being
> able to distinguish who was a stranger, and that made
> me extra anxious. Someone told my parents that
> having clear routines and spaces would help me to
> relax.

That makes sense. At our age, we need our routines.
On our holiday recently, I also went through that.

> Did you?

When I was introduced to someone, even though
they said it was my uncle or aunt, I was scared
because I hadn't seen them much. That passed, but
now I miss Mummy very much when she leaves
because I know that even though I don't see her, she
is still there somewhere.

> That's right. Anyway, the plan now is to go to nursery
> school in the morning. It works because I see other
> children. So my parents have now been able to
> reorganise their times. Now at home, that time during
> the afternoon or evening when Mummy is not with
> me, Daddy is always there. I see Grandma or Jenny,
> but either my mum or dad is always there.

Oh! That sounds better!

> And also when Mummy or Daddy go out, they always
> say goodbye and one of them always stays and in that
> way, we say goodbye together. It is a bit painful but
> it is better than that horrible feeling of when they

> disappeared and I didn't know when they would return.

Now, that's a great idea.

> Well, I still feel very upset. But this gives me more security about what happens around me. Also, the little while that I am with Mummy or Daddy, and when they bathe me, put me to sleep or give me dinner, they are really comforting.

I'm glad you feel calmer.

> Me too, what a relief! See you later!

What Is Happening Here?

Paul, four months, chats with his friend of six months and Teresa, aged eight months, talks to a girl of her age. Both in their own way explain their experience of what goes on around them, when they find it difficult to connect with the person who acts as their reference point due to the lack of opportunities. They feel lost in a complex world where the anchor points that steady them are failing, leaving them without the grips they need to do their climbing,

These stories have one thing in common: that children feel the loss of a sufficient and stable connection with their mothers, or with reference figures because they are busy. In one case the mother is at home, in the other, she comes and goes. In these cases, when the children see their mothers, their signals do not reach them with enough frequency and/or continuity to help them progress emotionally, as they require.

Paul's situation illustrates a lack of stimulation somewhat different from that of his friend, Beth. From his point of view, physically speaking, he sees his mother behind her mobile phone. Therefore, instead of having a face with all its expressive details and movements accompanied by smiles and sounds, he sees a metallic rectangle in between. If the infant's perspective, from his mother's lap, allows him to see even some of her face, still her eyes are not looking at him. From what he says, this seems to be a very frequent occurrence.

If the situation of Beth's little friend with his parents occurs very frequently during those times of the day when he is awake and they are together, it will have an impact on his emotional development. Paul has been losing magnificent opportunities at critical moments to learn from his mother's face and from her looks to hold "proto-conversations" in which there is time to "talk" and "listen" and also to "listen to oneself" and be aware of the reactions that this communication causes.

Probably Paul will be confused and will have to take refuge in the exploration of objects, in this case for reasons very different to Beth's. Not, as in her case, to take refuge in a situation where she has some control over something and to escape from excessive stimulation, but to obtain the stimulation he needs from his exploration of things. However, this will develop when Paul achieves more and better control over his hands. Meanwhile, this fragmentary emotional connection with his parents will probably increase his irritability and emotional distress.

In the first few months, we should be careful with the use of our mobile phone when we are with our babies because we must not forget that they establish their emotional connection mainly from our faces. In fact, we have a default template that works to direct our attention to anything that might look like a face: this template consists of two dots above and a line underneath, like a triangle. If we peer into the pram of a young baby "upside down", looking from their head downwards, the baby sees this pattern inverted, with the mouth at the top and the eyes below, and it is strange for them because they do not recognise it and sometimes this will cause the infant to pout.

Our second child, Teresa, tells us about another experience that, in the end, is related to a lack of stimulation since the stimulation that does take place is broken up and comes from different sources. Our destiny is to relate to many different people. But our origins lie in a very special relationship that revolves around one person. Based on our experience in this relationship, everything that comes afterwards unfolds and is amplified. Through this inter-subjective space with that special person, the baby crosses the threshold into the social territory, that of "the others", the "not-me", this special person is their bridge.

So, there is always a person that the baby prefers over others when they need comfort. This person is usually the mother because there is a prior history of gestation during which the mother develops a bond. This is coupled with the prenatal sensory imprinting as well as the smell and other experiences during birth. For Teresa, her mother is her primary caregiver, yet she sees little of her. It is not just a matter of shared time, but of Teresa knowing when this is going to happen, that there will be a certain routine so she can have the confidence that her mother will be there for her.

It is not ideal that the mother is totally absent for more than a few hours a day, especially in the first year. What Teresa is saying seems to refer to work trips that keep her away for two or more days at a time. This is too much because the little girl's time cannot be counted in the same way as ours is. That is why Teresa says that her uneasiness has been increasing since she is entering into the period of feeling fear when confronted with the strange.

When nearing the age of six months, structures in the brain mature that activate memory. It is a milestone in our individual history that is marked by several weeks during which it is possible to observe a kind of anguish before what is strange. The baby loses their blindfold and they will never be the same again, now the child can distinguish their mother and other people who are very close, from those they do not deal with or know.

Now that Teresa has a memory, when she is not with her mother, she misses her; furthermore, during these weeks when she is approached by someone she does not know and experiences this new sensation, she needs to turn towards her mother or shelter herself, and for her mother to reassure her.

If Teresa's situation continues with long and unpredictable separations from her mother and being looked after by several carers, her emotional development will be affected. She explains to her friend that she feels anxious and on continuous alert because she cannot control what is happening. If this situation continues and the stress she feels becomes chronic, it will physiologically affect the baby's body, which is undergoing full and rapid development, and also her brain architecture.

What she says has helped her feel better is that the chaos out there has been organised a bit during the hours she is awake in a way that substantially reduces her stress.

Now, she knows what is happening and what is going to happen and this gives her a certain calm because she is more in control, there is less uncertainty. When Mum leaves, now Teresa sees her leave and they say goodbye, knowing that they will miss each other but knowing that she is staying with the other parent, her father, who is equally responsible for her. To facilitate the new family organisation, Teresa spends the mornings at the nursery, which also sets a routine. Other people, like Grandma, are visitors but they are not central and take an appropriate place in relation to Teresa.

What These Stories Teach Us?

These stories teach us the importance of knowing the times and needs of our babies. The love we show is essential, but it is also essential to demonstrate that love in the way they need it and that is why we need to know their world better.

Today, we know that the best predictor of both their brain and socio-emotional development lies in the quality of the attention they receive from the person who is most emotionally significant to them. What is meant by "attention"? Among other things, *the warm attention to what happens to and what suits the baby, in a consistent way*. This attention favours the routines by which the baby gets a sense of things and also the effects they are able to cause on those things. Finally, *it is the kind of attention that gives the baby space and follows their pace.*

5
I Can't Explain Myself Properly Yet: Even I Don't Understand Me

We come to this life with a brain ready to structure itself in the image of the "world" into which we are born, precisely through its relationship with it. Emotions are powerfully assembled in the brain's most archaic structures; yet those emotions, with all their comings and goings, are also called upon to develop in other areas of that brain, to unfold themselves like a great rainbow. They will impregnate everything that we experience.

In our newborn, emotions, bodily sensations, pain, well-being... everything is mixed. From this kind of "primal magma", the process by which the infant can distinguish and identify what they feel is rather gradual. Furthermore, the process needs a wiser figure to attend to the child, who uses their words and figures out what may be happening in order to respond in different and appropriate ways. It is not an easy task for the parent, especially at the beginning, to know what is happening to their child, in their body and in their incipient mind, especially when the modes of communication are very limited and general. The most common message that they send to us is received, more or less, as "Oh! Something is happening to me... or maybe not?"

How is it possible to distinguish, for example, among feeling hungry, frustrated, bored, confused, uncomfortable, tired or overwhelmed? The first thing is the experience of feeling one way or another and then having the experience of opening out to the world in different ways. Thus, if they are hungry they are fed, if they are tired they are put down to rest, if they are sad they are distracted or comforted according to the circumstance, if they are anxious about an unknown situation they are calmed by being spoken to and touched, etc. In short, we read their signals, interpret what is happening and return to the infant our interpretation through our own actions. This will help them connect what is happening in their body to something from outside. Thus, their activation level decreases enough so they can organise and differentiate their own emotions.

Sometimes, this is a matter of trial and error and we have to try different interpretations. Often in this process, the child shows displeasure because we do not get it right and then we become more anxious. The situation generates a degree of stress in the mother or the father, who may take turns trying to figure it out.

With newborns, generally, the first thing that occurs to us is that the child is hungry and usually we are right since they are commonly fed between ten and twelve times a day, normally breastfeeding. It is a great relief when the baby stops crying while breastfeeding and, together with this relief we experience the satisfaction of the success of having given them what they need. Therefore, this "solution" is deservedly registered on the list of "star" options for the next sign of discomfort and crying. However, over time there is gradually more space for other emotions and sensations. There is a risk that we stay with our "star solution" and apply it to everything.

So, there are different emotions, feelings and sensations that the baby communicates but parents find them difficult to interpret, so they become perplexed. On the one hand, they are undecisive, but on the other hand, they are seeking a solution as quickly as possible. So they opt for the one that "works". Then, the communication moves as if it were in a funnel: varied signals end with a single response.

The stories of Luke and Karen illustrate these situations through their experiences that they share with their friends.

The baby boy has not yet reached three months and the baby girl is seven months old.

My Mother Has the Solution for All My Troubles

> Oh! I'm very confused... I don't understand anything.

You seem restless Luke... it's like you have all kinds of things tied up in a knot inside you. That happens to me too.

> I have only been here a very short time and sometimes I have such a craving in my tummy and I use code one. My mummy, who is very close to me, puts her breast to my mouth right away and the liquid I suck calms my tummy, and then I feel much better. After a few sucks, I can take little breaks and look at her.

That's called "hunger", I've been in this world longer than you and I've learned a few things.

> But then there are times when I am overwhelmed with so much novelty and I use code two and as soon as I turn around, I have Mummy's breast in my mouth; I'm not hungry, but I shut up.

But that's another thing that happens to you: even though things get mixed up inside there, one thing is hunger and the other is mental fatigue, and you say that you use two codes...

> Yes, but since I am new, I still haven't adjusted my crying tones well and I think that Mummy gets nervous, and she only has one thing on hand to stop me crying.

And do you stop crying?

> Well, with her breast in my mouth, I almost can't breathe, of course, I keep quiet... Sometimes I feel like I have sharp things sticking into me everywhere and I use code three, but before I have finished using it, my mouth is full up with my mum's breast. I think code three makes her even more anxious because I arch my back.

Of course, my friend, those are gases, like little sharp iron balls running inside our bodies, and suddenly sticking into us.

> That's it! That's what happens to me! And sometimes the problem is that I am bored, especially when I am tied into my rocker. There I also express myself as well as I can, and before you know it, her breast is in my mouth. And that's how it goes; I even use several codes in a row when I don't know what to do. And then my mum gets all confused and passes me from one breast to another, because she has two!

Now I see why you don't know what is happening to your body and you are so restless and confused. This is all about connecting what happens to us inside with something outside, which helps us to organise this sack of emotions we have. We are like black and white, on or off, yet really there is a wide range of colours, but to activate them we need a little outside help.

> Ahh! And how do I do it? I only have a few codes and not even I can tell them apart very well.

Well, let's hope that your mum will realise... it took my mum some time. I think someone was telling her a bit how we work, because after a while when I was tired, she would leave me alone and she whispered to me, and when I was frustrated and irritated, she would calm me down with some gentle movement…

> That makes sense! So little by little I could learn to distinguish what is happening to my body… Phew! I'm tired already (code two)… Oh no! Here comes my mummy, I can't talk anymore because she is going to plug me into her breast.

Good luck my friend!

I'm Always in the Air

Hello Karen, it's been a while.

> Yes, we haven't talked for ages.

How's it going?

> Well, almost worse than when we spoke the last time.

Gosh! What's happening?

> Well, there are lots of things that bother me or make me uneasy, and I get angrier without knowing why.

That also happens to me, the older we get, the stronger some emotions are.

> The thing is that as soon as I open my mouth and make the slightest grimace for whatever reason, I am up in the air in a flash!

Up in the air?

> Yes, my dad picks me up and since he is so big, it is as if I am flying until I land in his arms.

But that's wonderful, isn't it?

> I'm not so sure. Because sometimes it's my stomach I think, and it would almost be better if he passed his hand over my tummy without moving me because flying is not what I need when I'm feeling like that. The other day when I was landing, I was sick on Daddy's face!

What a face he must have been left with!

> Well yes… it was all a big drama because he couldn't see and I was in the air until Mummy came running. Other times, I complain because I think I'm overwhelmed and it is the same: they pick me up out of the playpen immediately and I'm up in the air again. So, maybe I am using code two and my father walks around energetically with me, moving me up and down, which is really irritating.

Well, I don't think that'll help you if you are feeling overwhelmed.

> Of course not! But how can I explain it to him, since I am not any good with CCG yet? So, I go into code three, kind of saying "enough, leave me alone!" and it makes things almost worse. Because he talks to me and he sings and makes funny faces.

Your poor daddy! It's complicated for parents… Sometimes it would be good to use an interpreter.

> It wouldn't be a bad idea! But a little patience for working out more solutions wouldn't hurt either.

I'm sure they have seen that sometimes picking you up has worked for you.

> Well, yes that's probably right. Since at the very beginning he picked me up and I calmed down, he has come to think that it's always right for everything. And on top of that Mummy thinks the same, and sometimes I go from Mummy's arms to Daddy's arms.

What happens is that we need to distinguish all the things that happen to us in our body, and that's really difficult if they always give us the same solution.

> Yeah, I'm sure. And now I'm getting even more confused. When I don't know what is happening to me, if they don't pick me up, I feel bad. The truth is that I'm not really sure why and although it seems to solve the problem for a moment, it only lasts a second, and in the end, I get very upset.

It sounds like what the grown-ups call a "vicious circle".

> Boy, you're sounding really classy!

It's because I'm a few months older than you, and the CCG is a whole new world. I spend all the time with my ears switched on and my eyes watching the grown-up's mouths.

> Oh! Well, to me that circle sounds like something that never ends! Code "Waaah!"

I'll let you go. They are coming to give me dinner now.

> See you soon… here we go, woooh! I'm flying again!

What Is Happening Here?

In these stories, Luke, who is less than three months old, talks to a six-month-old boy. Karen, who is seven months, also talks to another, somewhat older, a boy who is about eleven months old, he explains his great interest now in how grown-ups speak. The two protagonists tell us, in their own way, the frustration they feel in their communication processes with those who care for them. They experience varied sensations and emotions and signal them as well as they can. Out there, they find a quick answer but it is always the same one. *The parents receive indications of complaint or discomfort from their children and they respond immediately, but they do so without giving themselves a space to think and interpret what may be happening to the infants.*

Luke has a mother who had no previous experience of being with babies. She is the youngest of her siblings but has not had any nephews or nieces either. She feels a little insecure in her new role and insecurity is a strange sensation for her, since she is a woman who copes well in other areas of her life. The baby's crying upsets her because it is a situation that she cannot control. At first, in all the initial confusion because of the novelty of the situation, breastfeeding seemed to stop the crying instantly. But after a few weeks, she continues to offer a feed immediately when faced with any discomfort in her child, without stopping to examine what might be happening and whether it may be possible to respond to him in another way.

Luke's father, in his own way, also cooperates in this because any sign of complaint or discomfort in the baby is solved by taking him to his mother's breast, which seems to work.

If this situation continues, it will somehow consolidate itself because when Luke is older and is bored, he will leave his game and look for his mother's breast, and he will do so when he feels anxious too. *If his mother's breast becomes the solution, not only for feeding, but for everything, this will limit his knowledge of his own varied emotions and sensations.*

In the second story, Karen tells us about her father with whom she spends a lot of time. On the first day, when he went to put her in the Moses basket, his arms were shaking, partly because of the emotion and partly, since he was not used to doing this, with a feeling that he might drop her. As soon as she felt that insecurity in the descent backwards, Karen reacted with a reflex: she opened her arms and began to cry. Her reflex reaction was because she felt herself falling through the air, but he interpreted this as her not wanting to be left in the cot. *Karen's father has developed the conviction that the baby just wants to be in his arms and the situation now, after several months, feeds back on itself.*

Karen, now older, tells us that she is confused because now in any situation she cries to be picked up and this does not satisfy her either. Although it is good to have a baby in your arms, enjoying physical contact, they also need to rest and change position by stretching while lying down on a flat surface.

Karen's father is concerned that when he puts his daughter down to sleep, or anywhere else, she feels abandoned. Furthermore, these feelings are triggered when he hears her complain or protest. The intensity with which these feelings are activated in Karen's father points to his own story, which may be interfering in the handling of these situations with his little girl. He was adopted when he was a baby and although he feels very loved by his adoptive family, lately, since he became a father, sometimes he is surprised by these strong feelings about the possibility of his daughter feeling abandoned by him.

What these stories have in common, in terms of communication, is that the signal arrives and the mother or the father is fully there for the child. But when that communication arrives, the parents become restless and perplexed, and always respond in the same way. *They lack a proper attitude of interpretation.*

It is possible that, in some cases, in order to develop this ability to interpret the signals, parents need to find out if there is any reason that stops them from waiting and trying to find answers. It may be the need to perceive that the situation is under control, it may be some anxiety that is activated, it may be that we have the conviction that happy children never get upset. In any case, this pushes us to act immediately with whatever seems to stop the complaint or crying, it may be momentarily successful but not as healthy for the relationship and the emotional development of our infant.

Thinking about different things and trying them out requires us to tolerate a few moments of their displeasure and their crying while we find the most appropriate solution. In these circumstances, the main thing is to show confidence and stay calm because we are the ones in charge of the situation.

Stopping to explore exactly what may be happening and trying out different responses gives them some peace of mind, showing them that they are in good hands and with someone who knows what is best for them. If this is not the case, the situations are fed back and we enter into a trap, and the immediate "solution" becomes an obstacle to proper emotional development.

The child will find it difficult to distinguish between emotions, especially negative ones. Therefore, it will also be difficult for the child to develop ways of managing these emotions using differentiated strategies, as would be expected as they mature. This child will be confused and probably irritable and will have a hard time relating to other children and adults when these people do not respond immediately to what they want. When they are upset, they will be lost, because they have no practice in recognising what is happening to them and being content and soothing themselves based on the comfort they once experienced.

What These Stories Teach Us?

These stories teach us the importance of stopping to interpret what may be happening to our baby. *The important thing is to give differentiated responses to different sensations and emotions that the child presents to us in a very primal way.*

These stories also teach us that parenting requires us always to be alert to support and guide changes. Our actions have to be dynamic and in harmony with the complexity that is unfolding before our eyes, in a little person who is developing at a dizzying pace. Perhaps continuous change is the only constant that we encounter when we enter this job of parenthood. Knowing the keys to these changes helps us to better understand how to do a better job.

6
There's a Lot of Noise There. Can You Hear Me?

When a human being leaves the darkness to come into the light and takes the first breath of air, their story begins: everything lies ahead. The same happened to the people who made them possible and who precede them naturally on the road. They, like all humans who tread this Earth, also had that beginning. When a child is born, their history, which lies ahead, meets with the longer or shorter, luckier or less fortunate, history of their parents, a history that has made them who they are.

The life story of a human being is like a backpack. We all carry some weight, but some carry large loads, stones that accumulate and whose weight bends the back of the walker. So much so that sometimes they can only see their feet and little else, they cannot look at the horizon. They can only focus on the step that they are taking: just enough to be able to continue on the road.

The arrival of a child to parents with heavy backpacks often, in spite of the difficulties that may arise, renews their hope in the future. It is exciting to hear them say with all their hearts as they look at their baby 'I want to be a better person for this child'.

The arrival of a child is always an opportunity for parents to grow, but for some parents, this opportunity is truly unique. This is because that baby is someone who needs them and smiles at them. Their baby looks at them in a way that makes them feel unique and special. This is a very important feeling, one that perhaps they have been missing in their lives.

Therefore, feeling this way, tenderly needed and sought after, can give these parents a very special opportunity for personal development.

Children build their security, little by little, by communicating and feeling communicated with, in the eyes that look at them and return a certain sense of being. They express themselves as they are able and often have feelings of uneasiness that they do not understand. But gradually, everything will start to make more sense because out there is their special person who gives meaning to everything and transmits it to them. That special person is the interpreter of the world for them, the bridge that connects them with that world so they can visit it and know it, through their parent's eyes, gestures and words.

If the person who cares for and protects the child has a heavy backpack on their shoulders, this may cause interference when it comes to attending to and interpreting the infant's, sometimes confusing signals. Although the carer has achieved the merit of surviving and coping, in some parents the vulnerabilities that their history has left them may get activated in stressful situations, such as caring for a crying baby.

People are not always aware that the vulnerabilities left by their history of adversity can interfere with and complicate their parenting tasks. When a child does not find harmony and emotional coherence in their relationship with their mother, the development of their security and their progressive emotional self-regulation suffers.

The stories of Hope, Daniel and Anne illustrate these situations and experiences in their talks with their respective friends. The girl in the first story has just celebrated her first birthday. Daniel, in the second, is four months old and Anne, in the last one, is fourteen months old.

Mummy's Hope

We haven't talked for ages, Hope. I saw you this morning in nursery school, in the other class.

When?

When you arrived with your mum.

> Phew! Did you see me when I couldn't stop crying and screaming?

Yes… what was wrong with you?

> I don't know. When Mummy leaves, I always have a hard time because I can't stand it.

My mummy leaves too, but then she comes back.

> And how do you know?

Because I feel it like that. She has always been there and I know she is there, so I can concentrate on seeing the world.

> Well, my mummy too, but we don't seem to understand each other, and I don't understand myself either.

What do you mean?

> Oh, I don't know. When I was younger, sometimes I got scared.

Did you get scared?

> Yes, because she would cry and scream.

Just like that, out of the blue?

> No, when I put my hand in my food to see what it was like and then I wiped it on my face and discovered that I could make bubbles with my saliva. She said I didn't love her and she cried because of what I had done with the food that she had prepared for me.

So she didn't think your bubbles full of food were funny?

> No, you see it was quite an experience for me! But I was sorry and it scared me to see her like that.

My mother doesn't like it either, but she just wipes my face and says to me "Not now".

> Well, mine, after things like that, keeps quiet for a long time and then she comes and covers me in kisses. I didn't understand anything.

What a very kissy Mum you have!

> Yes, but I'm never sure how things are going to go. Sometimes it's as if she doesn't see me even though she is looking at me.

That must make you feel very insecure.

> It certainly does! When she goes away, I feel really bad. This situation makes me go to pieces. It's awful. I can only cry. And when she comes back then I'm so angry…

Poor you! Yeah, it's a mess. I also get sad when Mummy leaves but then I take a deep breath and since I know nothing is happening and there is so much to see and touch, I get distracted and have a good time until she comes back. So, then I tell her what I did and she is happy and tells me things too.

> Now I've started saying "NO" to some things.

Fair enough, it is about time for that. I do it too! We get older and we have to mark off our territory.

> Well, that gets me into all sorts of trouble. She gets angry and says she is not going to let me be pig-headed and make her life difficult... Pig-headed? Do you think our heads look like pig's if we say "No" too many times?

I hope not! But it seems that your mum takes things too personally, don't you think?

> Yes, I think so. The other day we went to see someone and Mummy was crying. Daddy was there too. I think she was talking about her bad feelings. I was playing in a corner but every now and then I would get up onto my dad's lap to see what was going on.

Well, maybe that helps her because it must be that she is carrying a great load and that is why she gets confused.

> That must be it... Of course, she was a little girl at one time, as well, I suppose... because mums and dads aren't born as mums and dads, are they?

Grown-ups are a confusing lot!

> You're dead right!

Let's see if things get better. See you soon!

> See you.

Bad Experiences

> I can't get any rest, I'm feeling really irritated!

What's wrong, Daniel?

> As soon as I fall asleep my mum touches me. She comes close, and when I open my eyes her big eyes are just an inch away from mine.

All the time, day and night?

> Yes, yes, day and night. You can't live like that! I think she's afraid that something will happen to me while I am asleep.

Poor thing. And you don't know why she does it. She must be exhausted too!

> Yes, she is really tired and bothered when she hears me protesting. And sometimes she complains to me too, as if I could do anything about it.

I also find my mum looking at me when I wake up… sometimes. But it has only happened a few times.

> I don't know if she looks at me beforehand, but she certainly wakes me up. And sometimes she has to take me in her arms because I don't fall asleep right away but then when I am asleep not a minute goes past without her moving me again and waking me up. I spend the day crying because I'm so tired and annoyed. And on top of that, she gets anxious and sometimes even cries.

Maybe she is afraid you won't wake up.

> Now that you mention it… in fact the other day I heard her cry, saying to my dad: "I don't want the same thing to happen to him…" but I don't understand. Daddy also gets annoyed with all these interruptions. He likes everything to be in order.

We don't know anything about how our mums' and dads' lives were before we arrived.

> What do you mean?

Well, my mum, for example, I heard that she told the doctor that before I arrived, she had waited for another baby who didn't arrive.

> The baby didn't arrive?

Yes, I don't know... Well, I suppose it stayed halfway. But I did arrive.

> Ah...

It is possible that in your case, another baby arrived, but then the baby left. And she was sad. That's why she doesn't want you to leave.

> I don't understand very well. But I'm not going anywhere. Let's see if she realises, because the way things are going, we aren't understanding each other.

I hope your mummy calms down and little by little she gets used to letting you sleep.

> Me too, I'll let you know.

My Two Dinners

Hi Anne! Are you having a snack?

> Yes! These biscuits are really tasty, it's my second snack!

The second?

> Yes, you see my mum wants me to grow big.

And do you have two dinners as well?

> Well, almost, yes. Because a little bit after my dinner I have a second round, a kind of "afters" of milk with loads of cereal before going to bed.

And isn't it too much?

> Well, the doctor lady we see always tells her that I've got too much of something…

Probably she's talking about weight.

> Oh yeah! That's it… weight.

And what does your mummy say?

> That when I am full, I'm calmer and rest more and she also feels calmer when she sees that I am full.

And are you walking already?

> Well, because I am so big, I drag myself and go on all fours, but getting up is very difficult. I'm not ready yet. Are you?

I can walk already, see!

> Wow! But we're the same age, how can you do it? It's not that easy, is it?

No, it's not easy. You have to think about lots of things: the weight of your bottom, with nappy included, your legs, one foot in front of the other… and all that without falling. You have to concentrate a lot to keep your balance.

> But it must be great to go around and snoop at everything... With a bit of luck and a good stretch, you must almost be able to open doors!

Yeah! It's great, and with your mum and dad chasing you... Ha! Just for that, it's worth falling as many times as it takes, even if it hurts... although sometimes the interruption is almost worse than the fall.

> I'm looking forward to it, but I'm not there yet.

Well, maybe if you only have one snack and one dinner instead of two, your bum will weigh less.

> That would help, but the only time Mummy and I understand each other well is at mealtimes... that's why I like them so much.

OK. Well, I'm going over there... walking! I have to concentrate! I'll leave you for now.

What Is Happening Here?

The three children in these stories, Hope, Daniel and Anne, have something in common: brave mothers who have suffered adversity in their lives. In order to understand the experiences these children tell to their friends, we need to look at the stories of these mothers because, as Daniel's friend says, "We don't know anything about how our mums' and dads' lives were before we arrived." They are stories of misfortune, and efforts to overcome them, that could happen to anyone.

Hope's mother, Maggie, has a history of adversity that has been a serious obstacle to her own life development. When she was six years old, while crossing the street with her mother, they were hit by a car. In a desperate effort to save her daughter's life, her mother gave her a big push, but she herself died in the accident. The impact of the loss, the terrible circumstances of it and the consequences on her life were enormous. For some time she was not aware that the situation was irreversible and her magical thinking made her believe that Mummy would come home if she behaved well.

At first, she stayed with her father and her older brother, who was eleven, but the depressed and desperate father escaped from his situation by abusing alcohol. Her brother blamed her for their mother's death, that day they had gone out because Maggie wanted an ice cream. They handled their terrible loss and their grief as best they could. Maggie suffered verbal and physical violence from both of them until when her father got married, Maggie, then aged 14, went to live with her maternal grandmother. She was not doing well at school. She spent many hours away from home, went with older kids, drank and smoked. She was attending a psychological support service at that time because her grandmother insisted, but she did not feel comfortable with it and soon quit.

When she was 20, Maggie met a boy, she went to live with him and shortly afterwards they had a daughter whom they called Hope. Her partner, aged 28, is a more stable man who has encountered fewer problems in his life than she has. Maggie has problems with depression, and in certain situations suffers anxiety attacks. Occasionally she resorts to drinking and also has asthmatic problems that are triggered by stress.

Maggie experiences motherhood as a hope of having a happier life, as a sort of renewal through having her own family. She feels she has been lucky with her partner because he can give her the stability she needs. Her good intentions are a start but her inner noise, her psychological discomfort, is a major interference when she tries to connect with her child. She is easily disturbed by the frustration of not knowing what her baby wants and she feels very inadequate.

In her own way, Hope tells of her experience of a fragmented communication with her mother that has made her feel insecure. When her child needs something that Maggie does not know how to interpret, she becomes anxious and she feels inadequate as a mother just at the moment when she most wants to do it right.

This generates a certain vicious circle because the little girl becomes more and more irritated and involuntarily contributes to the fact that her upbringing and care sometimes become a challenge that is difficult to overcome. Maggie may be overwhelmed by Hope's feelings because she has difficulty in managing her own anxiety.

What Hope tells at the end of her story is that they have asked for help and her father is with them. Maggie, who is carrying this heavy load from her past, needs someone to sit with her by the side of the road and help her to unpack the contents of her backpack, little by little. She needs to look at what she is carrying so she can reorganise it better. Being more aware of its contents and having it more organised will make the load lighter and the road easier. She will probably also need to learn how to attend adequately to Hope's attempts at communication with her. This will help her to reflect, in good company, on her feelings and those of her child.

Jenny is Daniel's mother. At 25 years of age, she has a history marked by various events that she has been able to overcome, but not without leaving part of herself in the process. Her parents separated when she was very young and her only memories of her father are from some photos. Her mother became involved in another relationship and soon another sister arrived. She had no contact with her father over the years and some time ago she learned that he had committed suicide.

The "new father", the only one whom she remembers as such at home, humiliated her frequently in favour of her half-sister and punished her with great severity. Jenny felt very angry because her own mother did nothing to protect her. Later, she realised that her stepfather used emotional blackmail on her mother.

Jenny's teenage years were very troubled and full of conflict and she was told to leave the house when she was 17 years old. For a year, she survived with the help of an aunt. She felt abandoned and any affectionate contact took her temporarily out of that frozen state which she felt inside. When she was 18, she became pregnant. She did not take care of herself and soon afterwards she lost the baby. At age 22 she became pregnant for a second time, as a result of a sporadic relationship. That baby died of cot death aged two months. This affected her greatly because she blamed herself for it.

Depressed, she began to meet up with an old friend with whom she started a relationship. Daniel was her third pregnancy when she was 24 years old. Jenny and Daniel's father had known each other since school days. They understood each other well and they had in common a feeling of being a bit like two lost souls who have come together.

Daniel's parents have suffered the effects of their many troubles, which have scarred them, leaving certain vulnerabilities. Daniel's mother has very little confidence in herself and tends to think that everything bad that happens is due to her clumsiness. The father is obsessive and when he is in situations in which he feels a lack of control he becomes very nervous. The two try to overcome their problems. Both are excited about Daniel and are determined for things to go well so he will have a happy childhood.

The experiences that Daniel talks about relate to Jenny's fear of losing her son. Losing a baby through cot death has scarred her, and seeing Daniel sleeping activates all her anxieties. This is understandable. *However, her lack of self-confidence now extends to her role as a mother and becomes a barrier to developing a fluid connection with Daniel, and this will affect her child's emotional development.* Daniel tells us that he has heard his mother talk to his father about her fears, and perhaps that will help her become aware of the extent to which her fears are interfering with her experiences when it comes to "tuning in" to her baby.

In the third story, Anne speaks to us. Her mother, Louise, is 30 years old and is overweight, a problem that is causing her diabetes. Louise has suffered in various ways throughout her life. From a very young age, she had different experiences of separation from her mother, who suffered from a chronic illness that required frequent periods of hospitalisation.

Louise was in the care of neighbours and various family members because her father had to travel for his work. She had a brother two years older than her, and sometimes they took him with her and sometimes not. Louise never knew when her mother was going to disappear and was always anxious and alert. When she returned, she would hold on to her and not move from her side. As she grew older, she understood that her mother would have to go into hospital. However, each time she left, Louise always thought she would never see her again.

When she was nine years old, during one of her mother's absences, a teenaged cousin sexually abused her. These episodes were repeated for a while, and although Louise never said anything she managed to avoid being left in that house.

From puberty, she began to have problems with food. Louise ate whenever she was anxious or sad or confused, and she began to put on weight. Due to her appearance, she suffered a certain rejection by her classmates but this did not seem to matter to her. She almost felt comfortable being left alone. She studied Administration and works in a large office as an administrator. At the age of 29, she became pregnant with a daughter from a fleeting encounter with a man she hardly knew; she was drunk and did not remember much about that night.

The news that she was expecting a baby, filled her with emotion and Louise is trying to raise her child on her own as well as she can. She does not have much help because her mother died, but her brother also has two children and she has a very good relationship with her sister-in-law. This is an important support for her.

What Anne tells us is that her special communication with her mother has been focused through food. It is like an island of calm and mutual understanding in the middle of a sea where there is more disagreement.

Concentrating all the pleasure of comfort and emotional connection around eating brings the risk of developing health problems associated with food. Anne is already beginning to be overweight. It is taking her a long time to start walking and because of this, all related experiences are being delayed. There is a cascading effect on other areas of development such as cognitive and socio-emotional development, as well as on her different emotions and feelings of tiredness, boredom, joy, relaxation, sadness, nervousness... All of these have a single answer: the satisfaction that comes from eating. There is a funnel effect. This stops Anne from exploring the diversity of experiences that deserve their different emotions.

Knowing the history of the mother, Anne's experience with food can be related to her mother's unfortunate background. This illustrates how the troubled story of the woman to which Anne has arrived as a daughter can affect the present situation. Thus, the effects of adversity in childhood are passed from one generation to the next. If Louise gets help, this trajectory could be changed in favour of a healthy emotional development for her little girl. So, Louise could also grow, thanks to her motherhood.

What these stories share in terms of communication, from the baby's perspective, is that their mothers are present and try to listen, but emotionally they feel a lot of internal "noise" that produces interference.

The doubts of Hope's mother about whether she deserves to be loved are the main noise for her. This makes her confuse what Hope does, or does not do, with the girl herself. That is why she reacts so negatively when she thinks that Hope is intentionally rejecting her in everyday situations, such as with food issues. The fears of Daniel's mother of abandonment and loss are the noise, in her case, that interferes with listening to what Daniel tells her. Finally, the experiences of loneliness, uncertainty and abuse, as well as taking shelter in food, are Louise's noise, which has distorted communication with her daughter Anne.

What These Stories Teach Us?

These stories teach us *the importance of our own emotional well-being in caring for and bringing up our children*. Therefore, they highlight the importance of taking care of ourselves when we know that, due to various circumstances, we have had to carry a weight that holds us back. Looking after ourselves is always necessary, but it is even more important if a son or daughter comes into our lives. Because, even if we have more or less survived up to that moment, parenthood by its very nature will shake us up emotionally, and we must be aware of it. *So life brings us not only a baby but also the opportunity to grow and come out stronger.*

7
Don't Push Me Too Much or Too Little... Just the Right Amount!

A baby's arrival awakens in their loving parents a great tenderness. Along with this tenderness, we also feel some uncertainty about our ability to carry out a life project of this kind. What kind of mother or father will I turn out to be?

All the sediment of our personal history, including our fears and desires, is stirred up almost without noticing it. If our memories are of a childhood during which we did not hear our parents say they loved us, then maybe now we think that every day we will tell our child how much we love them. We needed it when we were young, and we do not want what happened to us to happen to our child. If, on the other hand, as children, we felt overwhelmed by our parents' expressions of affection, we say that we will not be like this with our child. Thus, each of us, searching, could find some of the foundations of the main lines of their parenting project that relate to their own past.

Yet really the important thing is to keep in mind that this baby is ours, in a unique context and circumstances. In that respect, it has nothing to do with what we were, in the context of our own childhood and our own parents many years ago. Therefore, *we must be very alert in order not to let ourselves be carried away by our own story, making it prevail over what the baby communicates to us.*

The focus has to be on the child and on knowing what their needs are, according to their own characteristics and circumstances. Giving our child lots of kisses because we need them, but at a bad moment for the infant, interrupting what they are doing, when it is not kissing that the child needs at that time – they many even protest and push us away-; what does this tell us? Even though I have the best intentions as a parent, I am attending to my own needs. I do not realise that the child's need is different and that they are sending me signals that I do not respond to. So my love should take another form, showing the child that I echo their signals. It is important to emphasise that, to the child, the feeling of being heard gives them their place as a "someone" in the relationship. This requires us to spend time with them. *So it could be said that pace and space give a child a place in the world.*

At other times, the parent is very focused on naming colours and shapes, for example by showing a blue triangle, and the child looks at them or throws up their arms waiting to be affectionately received; the father or mother says "not now" and insists that the child pay attention to the blue triangle. Here we have the same situation. Perhaps the father, with his best intentions, believes that his daughter should concentrate on distinguishing colours and shapes because that way she will learn quickly. Maybe this parent has particular reasons to place a very high value on everything related to the world of the intellect. However, what matters at this moment is being with the child and tuning in to them emotionally, enjoying togetherness and having a good time.

So parenthood requires us to have our "receiver" tuned in to pick up the baby's signals. However, this alone is not enough because it is not only a matter of responding appropriately but also of leading by being a proactive guide, accompanying them in their increasing autonomy. In doing so, it is necessary to develop a good sense of the pace of the steps we take.

We can use an eloquent example: when the child stands up and begins to take their first steps. We stand in front of them to encourage their practice and progress. If we are positioned too far away, either the child makes an attempt and falls after a few steps, or does not try at all, or maybe they do the first of these and after the unpleasant experience of falling, they do the second. However, if we are positioned right next to our child, no progress can be made because there is no space to try to walk. Therefore, we have to stand neither too far nor too close: just at that distance that allows the child to move forward, and which allows us to ask for that little more when we feel the child can do it.

This image can serve as a general guide on how to act in all areas. We are there to mark the path for them, and by making the path practicable it will take them as far as they can go.

We cannot slow down the clock, because this would hinder their progress. We cannot speed it up, either, because our child cannot be given shortcuts: they have to dock at all ports. We must accompany our children in a way that is appropriate to their progression, without lurching between backward and forward steps.

The stories that George, David and Jessie share with their respective friends illustrate these types of situations that babies experience. George is six months old, David is younger and has just completed his fourth month, and Jessie is almost five months of age.

Mummy Wants Me to Be Her Baby Forever

Hi George! Still lying down?

>Yes, can you come closer so I can see you a bit better?

I'm already in my buggy and I am so excited that I go around in it clapping my hands.

>Wow, I would love that. My mummy and daddy carry me around all the time in their arms, like when I was very young, or lying down in the pram. So what I see

> most is the ceiling of the house or the sky when we're outside, and everything from below.

So why don't they take you out of your carrycot?

> No idea! My mummy is delighted with me and so is my dad.

So?

> Well, I've heard my mum saying she's really sorry I'm getting older.

But that's what happens! That's why we come here, to grow. It would be horrible if we always stayed little, and they passed us around like a parcel!

> Yeah, but it seems I'm not going to have any little sisters or brothers, or so I've heard. That's why Mummy wants her little baby to be like this forever…

Well, you're missing out, big time.

> You said it. I can't get my arms and hands to work the way I would like. Also, I feel very loose and I am really clumsy when it comes to picking up the things I see.

Of course, if you don't spend some time sitting up, which you should do at your age, you can't experiment and practice with your hands in the same way, and that is why they're all floppy.

> Also, I get bored. Well, I'd better let you go. We'll talk more another day because my neck hurts from turning to look at you.

OK, I'm sure our mums will go out together soon and we can see each other again.

***

What a surprise, George! Today you are in a buggy! And what a buggy, it's really cool!

> Oh yeah! I still fall to the side a bit, from lack of practice. That's why the buggy is tilted back a bit. But this is another world!

I told you, didn't I!

> You see everything differently, and what is more, I can see my hands with everything around, behind, above, below…

Tell me, what brought the change?

> My parents took me to a place where you play with things and they told Mummy and Daddy that I should be doing things that I wasn't doing, and that it was about time for me to be sitting up. There they mentioned moving me to a buggy and forgetting about the carrycot and the pram.

Well, I guess it wasn't easy for your mother to take that step…

> I think you're right. Everyone was talking for a long time… Then, my parents talked when they got home and I saw them put the carrycot away. That afternoon they began to sit me on the couch between them, with cushions. I couldn't believe it, and I did all the funny things I knew and had a great time.

Wow! Well, I'm very happy because now we can go about in our buggies looking around and talking about all the things in the world out there.

> That's right. After all, we are almost the same age.

You'll see how quickly you get up to speed.

> Yep, definitely. This is so great. Let's clap hands!

Cool! We are going to have such fun!

Mummy and Daddy Are Super-Proud of Me

Hi David! What a big smile!

> My mummy and daddy are super-proud of me. They say that I'm almost talking and that soon I'll start walking because I'm very smart. They already see me as if I were older.

But what do you mean, talking in CCG? You've just arrived... how long have you been around here?

> I don't know, I think they count it as four somethings...

Four months?

> That's it, four months.

Well for talking and walking you're not there yet, because to get there you have to do lots of other things first. You have a long way to go. But, step by step, not taking kangaroo jumps!

> Well, I reckon you're right about talking using CCG, I think they are getting ahead of themselves. I'm having difficulty with the "gugu" and "baba" stage, in spite of them saying it all the time to help me practice.

And what about walking?

> When they pick me up they put me on my feet on their knees. So I stretch because they give a satisfied face that is so nice to see. But I still feel all soft, and I get very tired very quickly.

Well that puts a lot of pressure on you.

> You're quite right. Sometimes I can't take it anymore and I get a sort of "blackout" up here. And then it seems they get worried.

The opposite happens to me. My mum says that she loves babies and we shouldn't grow up. The thing is that I've been in this world for more than six months and I spend most of my time lying down or, at the most, reclining. It's the same when we go out: I am just looking at the sky.

> Yep! Some go too far, others not far enough…

How right you are!

Older or Younger, Which Is It?

> I don't understand this world!

I don't get it either, Jessie. And I'm trying really, really hard!

> This is supposed to be about going little by little, doing things by ourselves.

Yes, but not too fast... or too slowly.

> You said it, exactly. Going "little by little" at our own pace. Well, for me it's not that I'm going too fast or too slow: it's that for some things they expect me to be older and for other things, younger. And it's all a big mess!

Em... I don't really understand you.

> Look, they always put me lying down, or at most tie me into the rocker, as if I were younger. And Mummy carries me around like a little baby, cradling me. Meanwhile, my friends of the same age are all sitting up, facing the world. And they also spend time on the ground, rolling around like sausages and kicking the air.

So, they are going too slow for what you need...

> Yes, but then they take me to the nursery and they expect me to behave like an older child, not eating until Mummy comes to give me my food that she has brought with her. I get moments when I start to feel faint because I'm not old enough to wait that long. Poor Mummy is so busy, sometimes she is late. But when she comes, I can only think about my milk, I don't even think about Mummy or anything else, and it takes a while for me to get over my irritation.

And in making you wait it's like they are making you go faster than you are able...

> That's right. Now, with those hungry spells I have at the nursery, at night I am sleeping very badly. I think it is like night has become day, because I am hungry really frequently, and since my mum is available right

next to me… I take the opportunity to feed, or just to suck because I also feel restless.

Well, that is definitely like a younger baby. But in the morning your mum must be very tired and you too!

Yes, we are tired. And not in a good mood.

At our age, resting with no interruptions at night time helps us to be fresh during the day, and at those times when we are not eating or napping, we can concentrate and learn from everything.

Well, in that, I can tell you now things aren't going well…

Well, very soon you'll start eating other, more varied things, so you won't need to starve because you can eat even if your mum is not around.

I hope so. But there is other stuff…

What stuff?

My parents want me to be very nice and smile when they take pictures or when I'm with family. And since sometimes I'm tired or confused I don't feel like it and I cry.

It can be really annoying, asking us to act up like that.

Well, I don't think they like me crying, because they look at me all disappointed. They say that I do it to upset them and that I am becoming unso… something…

Unsociable.

Insatiable?

No. Unsociable... which means you're not very social.

Ah right! Well... well, I don't like that strange word.

Well, forget about it then. The best thing for us is that they go at our pace. There are mummies and daddies who expect us to go faster than we can: it is like they are pushing forward, and there are others who seem to have the brakes on.

Yes, but in my case, it is that for some things they push, and for others they slow me down. That's why I'm so confused, and that's even with me trying very hard to adapt.

Yeah, that's even more of a mess!

What Is Happening Here?

George, David and Jessie, the children who tell these stories, describe their experiences when what their development and maturity ask for and the opportunities that are given to them are out of step. If we look at it in terms of expectations, we would say that with George, aged six months, the expectations are low and this is holding him back, while with four-month-old David, expectations are so high that judging from what his parents expect from him the child should already be turning one. As regards Jessie, aged five months, it is mixed because it seems that by day, she is expected to be older, as if she were ten months old, and at home at night, the routine is closer to that of a baby of two months.

George has a happy mother delighted with her motherhood. She has waited for this child for a long time. The delivery presented problems and she knows that she has lost the possibility of becoming pregnant again. She is still processing the grief that this loss causes her and to an extent time has frozen for her. It does not help her situation that George's father works in another city and spends very little time at home.

George is a healthy and strong boy who is maturing at a good pace, but out there, things are not going at the same rate. The experience he talks about, always lying down and with his mother taking him in her arms as if he were a newborn, should be considered the tip of the iceberg in terms of what is happening between the mother and him. She was an only child and always dreamed of having several children because she did not want her son or daughter to have the experience that she had, of not having siblings. So for the mother to know that she will never mother a baby again makes her suffer. Her way of dealing with it is by extending this period, pretending that George is not growing up.

In this case, George has arrived into his mother's life circumstances, which are potentially problematic for him and his proper development. It is essential for his development that George stops spending all his time lying down or tied into a reclined rocker. He needs to be helped to sit up, and he should be in a more vertical position when he is in her arms. This is not simply a matter of motor development.

Looking at the world while sitting up is a dramatic change in the perception and experience of space and one's position in it. For George, the vision and management of his own hands as closely positioned "characters" on a "stage" of objects and people also reorganises crucial developments in his mind. Furthermore, the child needs his mother to look at him and focus on his needs so that a good emotional connection can be established. Now, without a doubt this connection is suffering because the mother is concentrating more on what she needs. The changes that George mentions are positive ones and seem to indicate that the mother, with help, is in the process of overcoming her problem, becoming more focused on him in order to support him in his progress.

David's story conveys his parents' delight with him. This fascination is common and natural in parents when they look at and admire their baby. However, *if these feelings become unreal expectations regarding the child then perhaps their vision is coloured by their own aspirations. They do not see the child as he is, but as what they want him to be.* The parents are, therefore, connected with "their image of David", and not with him.

Both parents, but particularly the father, come from families in which affection has been subordinated to achievements: without success, you are no one. In their life histories, what you are, has not been emotionally separated from what you do. In some way, attributing extraordinary achievements to their child justifies their admiration for him. If this becomes a relationship pattern, it could seriously harm David's emotional well-being and proper development.

The hurry they are in, puts pressure on the child that puzzles him. Insisting on holding him on his feet, this tires him out but at the same time, he receives a big smile from his mother or father. There is no space for him to express himself and there is an insistence for him to repeat certain sounds. His overloaded brain "shuts the blinds" in order to be able to reset, and his misunderstood apathy and "lack of interest" frustrate the parents, and all this is felt by David. This is disorientating and emotionally confusing.

Jessie lives with her parents, who are quite busy. Her story illustrates a somewhat mixed situation. On the one hand during the day they ask her, as if she were older, to endure several hours without feeding and also to be nice to people when they ask her to. On the other hand, they take her everywhere lying down as if she were a very young baby and at night time Jessie breastfeeds on demand.

Neither one nor the other is a problem if it is at the appropriate age. For example, if Jessie were a month, or a month and a half old, depending on her weight, it would be appropriate for her to be fed on cue, day and night. On the other hand, if the girl were a year old it would also be appropriate and expected to follow some social indications such as saying goodbye and waiting a while between meals, etc. But Jessie is six months old and is too old to be carried around like a young baby, and she is too young to be asked for things, and for people to get upset because she does not respond. Hence her confusion, which does not favour her balanced emotional development.

Jessie's parents have read a lot about parenting and have different opinions about what their girl's future should look like, how her schooling should be, etc. They spend time talking about it, but in their daily affairs, they get caught up in whatever is happening at that moment and respond to specific situations losing sight of the whole. They are busy and become trapped in their routines so they do not realise that they need to make changes to adapt to Jessie's needs, which are also changing. That, in part, explains the incoherence. In addition, the mother wants her daughter to live in freedom, to have a life different to her own experience of a strict home, and she tries to apply this at night when she is at home. If the situation is not reorganised and this incoherence persists, Jessie's irritability and resistance will only increase. As the months go by, she will have problems managing her negative emotions, such as anger.

What These Stories Teach Us?

These stories teach us the importance of being aware of the baby's development in order to make the necessary changes in that process, always with reference to the infant and always at a pace acceptable to the child. Pushing the right amount, neither too much nor too little.

These stories also teach us that having a child must involve considering our parenting project and how it is integrated into our life and personal development. Reviewing our history as children makes us aware of where we come from. However, in this project, the core must be the child, their characteristics and their needs. *Our actions should be oriented to provide them with the guidance they need to become an independent person. For this, a good knowledge of the baby's world is necessary.* Our personal life stories will undoubtedly colour our performance as parents. The key is for them not to prevail over the reality and the needs of our baby, in that child's own context.

Recapitulation

In these pages, thanks to our shared codes, we have created the illusion of sneaking, almost on tiptoe, into a world where babies communicate with each other and have their chats about how their lives with us are going. Really, this stage of life is a fascinating world. Moreover, it can make us realise how very lost many of us parents can become, trying to handle our own adaptation as well as theirs, which moves at a dizzying speed.

The journey we have made has shown us the variety of situations in which, due to different circumstances, the signals of our babies do not arrive correctly. We have seen circumstances that stress and reduce our limited human attention span, such as a conflict within a couple, or a sick family member; situations that we have suffered and left in us traces that interfere with our listening abilities; perplexity and anxiety due to a lack of understanding of what is happening for our babies; grand dreams for our children which, like clouds, stand between us and the reality of their needs; physical absences from children's lives that they do not handle well…

Being aware of how a baby's mind emerges and how it develops emotionally is a great help with our parenting. What does not help is to be naive, thinking they are so young they are not really aware of anything and only need to have their basic needs covered: eat, sleep, and they will grow and then we will give them the best education. It does not help either to think that a happy child, our baby, can never be upset and that they know what they want and what suits them. Growing in all senses includes regulating the negative emotions that must be experienced to learn how to manage them. Knowing all this is essential so that during the intense emotional relationship with our baby in that first year of life we can help to build the foundations of their security. In short, we can be for them a wonderful and life-giving shadow like that provided by a leafy tree.

The emotional importance of the change produced by parenthood, whether with a first child or a third child, is clear. The stress associated with these processes is also obvious. When an adult is experiencing a change in their life, one involving a redefinition of their identity and roles, it would be important for that person to have the support that facilitates making this transition safely. However, if the adult undergoing this change is parenting a baby that is completely physically and emotionally dependent on them, this support is not just desirable but essential.

The current knowledge of early brain development, with its potential but also its vulnerabilities, today makes it irrelevant and obsolete to talk about parents who need support and parents who do not need it. These phenomena highlighted above occur in all parents and involve all of their babies.

The stories these babies have told us, all inspired by real cases, illustrate the very diverse circumstances of life. They also show how changeable these can be.

A mother can start by being "over-present" and, a few weeks later, suffer a very stressful situation such as the illness of a family member. So now, she is not focused when she is with her baby, due to her worries and distress. In the same way, a mother who has a good relationship with her baby and has an attentive presence, a few months later can experience a serious conflict with her partner that affects her attention and communication with the baby. These kinds of changes affect the emotional well-being of children. *Since life is changing, that is why it is so important to take care of the caregiver, in order to protect the proper emotional development of babies.*

All the information that accompanies these stories is in line with what is currently known about early development, particularly focusing here on the first two years of life. We are fortunate because in recent decades there have been impressive scientific advances in this area. This has been possible thanks to a dynamic of multidisciplinary interconnection involving several different areas, for example, Developmental Neuroscience, Psychology and Prevention Science. These synergies have produced important theoretical and applied developments.

We are all surprised at the rapidity of the changes we see in the early period, especially in the first thousand days approximately three years of human life. Yet understanding these kinds of changes and the ways in which they occur are relatively recent scientific achievements.

On the threshold of the 21st century, the US National Research Council and the US Institute of Medicine, sensitive to the effervescence in this area and its great potential to advance human development, commissioned a committee of experts to review and collate what was known about the nature of early development and the role of early experiences. The committee was chaired by Dr Shonkoff, Professor of Paediatrics at Harvard Medical School and Director of the Centre on the Developing Child. Its goal was to obtain an image, with a scientific basis, of the most important achievements of early childhood and environmental conditions that promote or hinder these achievements.

The results of this work were published in a volume in the year 2000[1] by Dr Shonkoff jointly with Dr Deborah Phillips, Professor of Psychology and Co-Director of the Centre for Research on Children in the US at Georgetown University. The contents explicitly indicated the recommendations and implications derived from it to be used for the benefit of babies in all areas: by those responsible for social and childhood policies, professionals, researchers and the parents themselves.

---

[1] Shonkoff, J. P. and Phillips D. A (2000) *From Neurons to Neighborhoods. The Science of Early Childhood Development*. National Academic Press, Washington D.C.

What stands out in this situation is that we now have a better understanding of the importance of early experiences in brain development and its role, as a support or an obstacle, in the appropriate adaptation of the child. Almost two decades later, our knowledge continues to grow. This knowledge gives us a broader view about how early experiences affect all aspects of development and in particular how the development of emotional security fosters the child's learning in the school setting and their capacity to relate with peers.

The relationship with our babies can benefit from this knowledge, based on which this book has been written and in which technical terms have been deliberately avoided. These terms are nothing more than abbreviations that work as labels to facilitate communication between professionals. What has been poured into these pages are precisely the realities that underlie the existence of these labels (e.g. emotional security in "secure attachment").

An appropriate response to a baby's signals requires that we be attentive, but also in charge of the situation, moving between what we ask and what we give, in a dynamic of helping them to develop their emotional self-regulation. Being attentive, in order to answer and to offer, depends on knowing how to listen, in a broad sense. For that, it is essential to know at least a little bit about those we are listening to babies. This book aims to contribute to that knowledge. Finally, responding appropriately and promptly to our baby also requires us to be at peace with ourselves and to take care of ourselves emotionally, being aware of the importance of this for the well-being of our babies.

If we are carrying a heavy burden, then parenthood can be a good time to put our emotional affairs in order and thus stop the burden's effects being transmitted to our children through our difficulties in communicating with them. Our children will develop the security they need to, and feeling that good shadow of the great tree that we are for them, they will venture to explore the confines of the wide world that calls them. We can also experience the personal growth that goes with accompanying them and guiding them on their journey through life.